Cliffs

Their Eyes Were Watching God

By Megan E. Ash

IN THIS BOOK

- Learn about the life and background of Zora Neale Hurston
- Preview an introduction to *Their Eyes Were Watching God*
- Explore the novel's themes and character development in the Critical Commentaries
- Examine in-depth Character Analyses
- Acquire an understanding of the novel with Critical Essays
- Reinforce what you learn with CliffsNotes Review
- Find additional information to further your study in the Cliffs Notes Resource Center and online at www.clffsnotes.com

WILEY

Wiley Publishing, Inc.

About the Author
Megan Ash is a graduate of the College of Education at Ohio University. She teaches English and communication at an Ohio high school.

Publisher's Acknowledgments
Editorial
Project Editor: Michael Kelly
Acquisitions Editor: Gregory W. Tubach
Editorial Administrator: Michelle Hacker
Glossary Editors: The editors and staff of Webster's New World™ Dictionaries
Production
Indexer: York Production Services, Inc.
Proofreader: York Production Services, Inc.
Wiley Indianapolis Composition Services

CliffsNotes™ *Their Eyes Were Watching God*

Published by:
Wiley Publishing, Inc.
909 Third Avenue
New York, NY 10022
www.wiley.com

Table of Contents

How to Use This Book

CliffsNotes *Their Eyes Were Watching God* supplements the original work, giving you background information about Zora Neale Hurston, an introduction to the novel, a graphical character map, critical commentaries, expanded glossaries, and a comprehensive index. CliffsNotes Review tests your comprehension of the original text and reinforces learning with questions and answers, practice projects, and more. For further information on Zora Neale Hurston and *Their Eyes Were Watching God,* check out the CliffsNotes Resource Center.

CliffsNotes provides the following icons to highlight essential elements of particular interest:

Reveals the underlying themes in the work.

Helps you to more easily relate to or discover the depth of a character.

Uncovers elements such as setting, atmosphere, mystery, passion, violence, irony, symbolism, tragedy, foreshadowing, and satire.

Enables you to appreciate the nuances of words and phrases.

Don't Miss Our Web Site

Discover classic literature as well as modern-day treasures by visiting the Cliffs Notes Web site at www.cliffsnotes.com. You can obtain a quick download of a CliffsNotes title, purchase a title in print form, browse our catalog, or view online samples.

You'll also find interactive tools that are fun and informative, links to interesting Web sites, tips, articles, and additional resources to help you, not only for literature, but for test prep, finance, careers, computers, and the Internet too. See you at www.cliffsnotes.com!

LIFE AND BACKGROUND OF THE AUTHOR

Personal Background

According to a bit of folk wisdom that Zora Neale Hurston may have known, "You can take the boy out of the country, but you can't take the country out of the boy." In this case, for *boy*, read *girl*, and for *girl*, read Hurston. Throughout her professional career as an anthropologist and writer, as well as her personal life, Hurston never really left the little country town of Eatonville, Florida, and its environs. Writing at a time when "local color" was out of fashion as an ingredient of worthy literature, Hurston's writings were rich in local color, and the front porch of Joe Clarke's Eatonville store became Hurston's symbol of hometown security. That setting could easily have been the place that Robert Frost described when he wrote, "Home is the place where, when you have to go there, they have to take you in." Eatonville was that sort of home for Hurston, but she did not ask Eatonville to "take her in." Instead, she took Eatonville into her life and kept it there.

The Early Years

The date of Hurston's birth is open to question. According to her, she was 9 years old when her mother died. The 1900 census report, however, which lists all members of her family, gives her year of birth as 1891. For reasons of her own, she gave the public the year 1901. She died on January 28, 1960. In between were 69 years of an extraordinary life.

Life for Hurston began in Eatonville, the setting of *Their Eyes Were Watching God*. Incorporated in 1866, this small, all-black town, about five miles north of Orlando, is located on the road that connects Florida Highway 17 and Interstate 4.

Biographers, including Robert Hemenway, must rely on Hurston's own story of her childhood as she tells it in *Dust Tracks on a Road* (1942). Hers was a carefree, rough-and-tumble childhood lived as children should live, at least until her mother's sudden death. Perhaps because Hurston grew up without a lot of mothering, she became a strong, vigorous, independent girl who did not back off from fights with her brothers and other boys. She climbed trees to look at the horizon, just as Janie does in this novel, and she knew the different scent of blossoms and various colors of foliage in her yard.

As a youngster, Hurston loitered at Joe Clarke's store in Eatonville as much as she dared, listening to men talking, absorbing their tall tales and stories and filing them away for future use. As an adult, wherever it seemed as though she would stay in one place for a year or more, she always planted a garden of flowers, greens, and beans. Perhaps this habit was a carryover from the large gardens that helped her parents, John and Lucy Hurston, feed their family of eight children.

Family Life

If her parents had marital problems, Hurston never elaborated on them. The closest she came to baring paternal infidelities is reflected in her first novel, *Jonah's Gourd Vine* (1934). A major character in the novel is, like her father, a popular pastor of a small Baptist church and a man who is attractive to the ladies in the church. Lucy Hurston, Zora's mother, was a small, frail woman. However, she was quite capable of managing her husband, as well as her children. Although he was an assertive, three-time mayor of Eatonville, John Hurston never stressed education. Lucy, on the other hand, encouraged Hurston and the other children to "jump at de sun." Like Janie's Nanny, Lucy was ambitious for her children.

Lucy's death was half of a double trauma for Hurston. When Lucy was dying, she asked Hurston to reject two folklore traditions: her pillow was not to be removed from under her head, and the clock and mirror were not to be draped. These requests were heavy burdens for the child. Needless to say, the women of the town always followed tradition, and little Zora was told to disobey her dying mother's last requests. As a result, Lucy left a distraught daughter, one who would carry a bothersome sense of guilt for many years.

The other half of Hurston's trauma was her father's rather hasty marriage to a woman who rejected his children. Hurston and her sister Sarah had been sent to a school in Jacksonville, Florida, but Sarah pleaded homesickness and returned to Eatonville. It was Sarah who wrote to Zora that their father had remarried. Whenever Hurston was home, squabbling between her and her stepmother continued, and several years later, the miserable situation finally culminated in a pitched battle between Hurston and her stepmother. Experienced from many fights with her brothers, Hurston easily won. However, she realized later that, during the fight with her stepmother, she was well on her way to killing the woman, a fate that Hurston believed that the woman deserved.

Work and School

Hurston describes herself as a student who always kept an inner privacy. She was something of a loner, and that inner loneliness may have been part of the baggage she carried with her when she left school, presumably to follow her mother's advice to "jump at de sun."

Hurston's first real job was far from the sun. She worked for about a year and a half as a maid to a performer in a traveling Gilbert and Sullivan company. When she left that job, she continued her education, first at the secondary school division of Morgan Academy in Baltimore (graduating in 1918), and later at Howard University in Washington, D.C., for five years. With limited employment opportunities, Hurston worked as a waitress and manicurist, barely supporting herself on the average income of twelve to fifteen dollars a week at Howard. However, in spite of the economic hardships, these were happy and challenging years for Hurston.

Career Highlights

From the time Hurston submitted her first story, "John Redding Goes to Sea," in 1921 to *The Stylus,* Howard University's literary club, until decades later, when she wrote a query letter to a publisher in the quavering hand of an old woman, Zora Hurston was a writer. If Hurston could have spoken to Alice Walker as Walker searched for her grave, Hurston might have said, "Remember me as a writer."

The Renaissance Writer

From *Dust Tracks on a Road,* we learn that Hurston gave the Howard University campus newspaper, *The Hill Top,* the name it still carries. At Howard, she became part of an exclusive literary group that included prolific writer and renowned educator Dr. Alain Locke. After her story, "Drenched in Light," was submitted to *The Stylus,* she sent it to Charles S. Johnson in New York City. As editor of *Opportunity,* he was looking for young writers, was impressed, and published it. Johnson also published another of Hurston's stories, "Spunk," and these two appearances in print fueled her desire to go to New York City and try her luck as a writer.

Only someone like Hurston would have had the courage to arrive in New York with no job and only a dollar and a half in her purse. She had friends, though. Earlier, she had met Johnson and his wife at Howard, and she paid tribute to Johnson and his support of young writers in *Dust Tracks*. She wrote that Johnson, through his editorship of *Opportunity* and his support of young black writers, really started the so-called *Negro Renaissance.*

The Negro Renaissance occurred during the 1920s, with Harlem known as its "culture capital," according to James Weldon Johnson. Since the community of Harlem in New York City became recognized as the center of the Negro Renaissance Movement, many refer to it also as the Harlem Renaissance Movement, sometimes also referred to as the New Negro Movement. During this time period, writers, poets, artists, musicians, and dancers gathered to share their talents and to tell the stories of the Negro experience. Such well-known figures as Johnson, Claude McKay, Countee Cullen, Langston Hughes, and Wallace Thurman flourished during the Harlem Renaissance. Hurston is associated with the Harlem Renaissance because she was in New York City during that time period. The Great Depression caused many of the writers and artists to leave Harlem to find other sources of income.

In New York, Hurston made friends easily, and it wasn't long before she was part of literary circles that included Margaret Walker, Claude McKay, Arna Bontemps, Aaron Douglas, Jean Toomer, and Langston Hughes. Her involvement with these writers and artists, as well as editors and publishers in the Harlem Renaissance movement, quickly earned her a reputation as an entertaining storyteller, sometimes to the despair of these new Negro artistic and literary elite, who often found her earthy style displeasing. Hurston didn't care; she kept on being herself. It wasn't long before Fannie Hurst, a successful and popular novelist of that era, offered Hurston a job, and another benevolent friend helped her to get a scholarship to Barnard.

Anthropology, Folklore, and Godmother

English literature had long fascinated Hurston as a possible college major, for she had been an avid reader as a child, but it was anthropology, with considerable help from Dr. Franz Boas, that Hurston finally chose as her major field of study. She emerged from Barnard a part-time writer and a full-time anthropologist, and Dr. Boas found grant money to support his student while she spent four years in the field gathering folklore. This collection of folklore provided models or precedents for the work she was doing, and she made mistakes in both her methods and her written reports.

Ultimately though, Hurston grasped what she was attempting and organized her material into *Mules and Men,* published in 1935. She focused on recording the tales told by the men on Joe Clarke's store porch in Eatonville, as well as stories she heard in the saw mills, turpentine camps, jook joints, and anywhere else that people gathered to relax and talk.

Like poet Langston Hughes and the artist Miguel Covarrubias, Hurston accepted the patronage of Mrs. Rufus Osgood Mason, whom she called Godmother. With more thought of her immediate needs than of her professional future, Hurston signed a contract that gave Mrs. Mason complete control over her literary output and its contents, including her research writings.

Hurston's Stories on the Stage

In 1931, Hurston had an unfortunate misunderstanding with Langston Hughes over the rights and authorship of *Mule Bone,* a play that they had hoped would be a collaborative effort. The bitter dispute severed their friendship. The 1991 edition of *Mule Bone* (Harper Perennial), edited by G. H. Barr and H. L. Gates, contains the complete story of the *Mule Bone* controversy.

With more zeal for her folklore than practical theatrical knowledge, Hurston launched into theatrical ventures to try to do alone what she had not been able to accomplish with Hughes. She was distressed that blacks were too often presented as caricatures onstage. She did not see what she considered to be honest presentations of the sort of people and lifestyles that she loved. She had no interest in acting, but she did want to try her hand at writing, casting, and producing. The odds were risky: Her knowledge of folklore far outweighed both her knowledge of the theater and her ability to get along with men and women in academia.

In January 1931, Hurston contributed three sketches to *Fast and Furious,* a revue that ran for a week and closed. Her next effort was *Jungle Fever,* a project for which she cared so much that she held rehearsals in her apartment and worked with a cast of Bahamans, including men with nicknames like Stew Beef and Motor Boat. Later, she used this play's storyline in subsequent theatrical efforts, including *The Great Day,* which was presented for a one-Sunday-only performance in January 1932.

Hurston attempted a collaborative production with Hall Johnson, whose reputation as a choral director was established. The arrangement came apart, however, because of differences in philosophy. Johnson favored concert arrangements of spirituals, and Hurston wanted simple folk arrangements. As happened with Hughes, Hurston later claimed that Johnson preempted some of her material to use in the concluding scenes of his *Run, Little Children.*

These theatrical projects brought Hurston offers to do dramatic work at Bethune-Cookman College in Daytona Beach, Fisk University in Nashville, and North Carolina College for Negroes in Durham. None of these commitments was successful, though, partly because of Hurston's intense dislike of academic life.

Enthusiasm has never been a substitute for experience, and Hurston's naiveté about the theater and her lack of contacts with theater people who had money and knowledge limited what she could do. Her efforts had been self-fulfilling, but they brought her no financial gains and made no lasting impression on the American stage. Unfortunately because of problems with ownership and production rights, her dramatic writings and musical scripts are not available to the public.

Back home in Florida, penniless as usual, Hurston became a writer for the Florida Writers Project, an extension of the Works Progress Administration (WPA) programs. For whatever nebulous work she did, she was paid $67.50 a month, bare sustenance wages even in 1935. She worked briefly on a research task with Alan Lomax for the Library of Congress, and this project would be her first foray into research in Florida. Afterward, she settled in Haiti, where she wrote *Their Eyes Were Watching God* in seven weeks. The novel roughly parallels Hurston's moving but hopeless romance with a delightful younger man who may have been the prototype for Tea Cake. Later, Hurston sailed to Jamaica, and *Tell My Horse* was the result of the research that she did there.

Was Hurston ahead of her time in her writings, or was she, as one of her characters puts it, "a mite too previous"? Although publication many years after one's death does not bring a promise of wealth or an audience for any writer, there are more opportunities for black female writers today than were open to Hurston while she was alive. She makes no mention of ever working with a literary agent, an intermediary that any post-Hurston writer would find essential. When the feminist (or, as Alice Walker prefers, womanist) critics, led by Walker, reintroduced

Hurston's work to the public's attention in 1975, they opened not just a narrow path to Eatonville, but a broad national highway for black female writers to travel. Hurston would have reveled in their journeys.

Fading Tracks on a Dusty Road

Seraph on the Suwanee, published in 1948, was Hurston's last novel, and it was far from successful. The failure of the novel, however, was not the worst disaster for Hurston that year. In September, a month before the novel was published, she was wrongfully accused of sexually abusing a mentally handicapped 10-year-old boy. She was not even in New York City at the time the alleged act supposedly took place. Although the charges were false, and she was exonerated, the damage had been done rather viciously by a Harlem newspaper that had printed information leaked from confidential court records by a court employee.

Hurston returned to Florida to work at whatever jobs she could find and to continue to do freelance writing for a variety of publications. She also did research for a novel that would be based on the life of Herod. For a while, she worked as a maid, and she was also a librarian at a military installation, making $1.88 an hour. Characteristically, Hurston did not get along with the other employees, and she was soon fired.

The dusty Florida road that Hurston traveled was nearing an end, a point at which the traveler sees the sign "No Outlet." In her later years, she gained weight, and she suffered a stroke in 1959. She died on January 28, 1960, in the St. Lucie County Welfare Home, in Fort Pierce. Her family, friends, and neighbors took up a collection to pay for her funeral and burial in an unmarked grave in the black section of the Garden of the Heavenly Rest, a segregated cemetery.

In 1973, novelist Alice Walker set out to search for Hurston's grave. As nearly as she could determine, she found it and had a plain, gray headstone placed on it, engraved with a phrase taken from one of the poems of Jean Toomer, "A Genius of the South." The resurgence of interest in the work of Zora Neale Hurston can be largely attributed to the attention that Walker has given it.

Eatonville Honors Hurston

Decades after her death, the Association to Preserve the Eatonville Community, Inc., established the Zora Neale Hurston Street Festival of the Arts and Humanities. The affair is generally scheduled for the last weekend in January and usually runs from Thursday afternoon through Sunday afternoon. The program includes a great variety of events related to the humanities. These include a juried art show, theatrical performances, and workshops for adults and children, dances, crafts, booths, and displays, and a multimedia exhibit of Hurston and her Eatonville roots.

Inquiries about the festival may be sent to: Zora Neale Hurston National Museum of Fine Arts, 227 East Kennedy Boulevard, Eatonville, FL 32751. Also, inquiries may be sent via e-mail: zora@cs.ucf.edu.

A list of Hurston's writing is much longer than most people expect. She published four novels, two collections of folklore, dramas, an autobiography, and many short stories and freelance articles for various newspapers and magazines.

INTRODUCTION TO THE NOVEL

Introduction

Hurston tells Janie's story in the form of a *frame*—that is, the author begins the novel and ends the novel with the same two people in the same setting, with only an hour or two having elapsed. Sitting on the steps of her back porch, Janie tells her story to her friend Pheoby Watson. The telling takes only part of an evening; Pheoby arrives at Janie's house in the early evening, and it is dark when she leaves to go home. Within this comfortable setting of one friend talking to another, Hurston tells Janie's story. This frame becomes the first part of the structure of the novel. The rest of the story proceeds chronologically, but it is not a first-person narrative. The author quickly takes over the telling and uses third-person point of view. The reader follows the experiences as Janie lived them, but it is the novelist who controls the story.

Within the frame, the novel has four units. First, Janie's early years with her grandmother. Second, an interlude where Nanny tells her own story and the reader learns about Janie's loss of childhood and the brief months of her first marriage. Janie's years with Joe Starks fill a third section, with the episode of the mule as an interlude that has no function in the story other than to show Janie's compassion for an ill-treated animal and an act of kindness that Joe did for his wife. Of course, it also gave Hurston an opportunity to poke fun at local customs, especially funerals. And the final section focuses on Janie's marriage to Tea Cake Woods. One interlude in the final section focuses on Mrs. Turner, and it serves to contrast Janie's open-mindedness with Mrs. Turner's bigotry. The frame is finally complete when Janie comes full circle and rests her tired feet on her own steps and spends the evening with Pheoby.

Within the framework of the novel, it appears that Hurston included many similarities that paralleled her own life. Like Janie, Zora grew up without much mothering. Her own mother died when Hurston was quite young. The character of Nanny in the novel seems to parallel Zora's own mother, Lucy Hurston. Like Nanny in the story, Lucy wanted her children to do well in life; she held their ambition for them, just as Nanny did for Janie.

One of the prevalent characters in the novel is Joe Starks, Janie's second husband. This character exemplifies an obvious similarity to Hurston's own life: Joe Clarke owned a store in Eatonville while Hurston was growing up there. As a child, Zora spent a lot of time there, listening to the men telling their tales. Both the store and the group of gossipers can be found in the novel. Joe Starks, in the novel, owns the crossroads store, and the men and women who gather to exchange stories are known in the novel as the porch sitters. Also, the character of Joe Starks resembles Zora's own father. He was a three-time elected mayor of the town of Eatonville, Florida, just as Joe Starks was in Hurston's story.

Janie's romance with a younger man, Tea Cake, also seems to parallel Hurston's life. Hurston also had a relationship with a much younger man, who may have served as the model for Tea Cake.

Eatonville, Florida, the setting of the novel, is an actual town located five miles north of Orlando. It is the oldest surviving incorporated municipality in the United States. Of the more than 100 black towns founded between 1865–1900, fewer than 12 remain, one of which is Eatonville. Perhaps it was the profound impact of this southern community on her life that prompted Hurston, who was born in Eatonville, to use it as the setting of this novel.

Hurston penned *Their Eyes Were Watching God* in 1937, a time when novels written by African-American female authors were rare. Not only was it unusual for an African-American female author to have a novel published, but also it was uncommon for novels written during this time period to contain an African-American female as a novel's heroine. Perhaps that is why many of Hurston's writings were overlooked until after her death. Noted author Alice Walker, who searched and found Hurston's unmarked grave in August 1973, reintroduced the public to Hurston's work in the mid 1970s. Through her writing, Hurston served as one of the first African-American female voices of the twentieth century.

A Brief Synopsis

This novel is the story of Janie Crawford's search for love, told, as noted earlier, in the form of a frame. In the first few pages, Janie returns to her hometown of Eatonville, Florida, after nearly two years absence. Her neighbors are curious to know where she has been and what has happened to her. They wonder why she is returning in dirty overalls when she left in bridal satin.

Janie tells her story to her friend Pheoby Watson, and after the story is over, the novelist returns to Janie's back steps. Thus, the story, which actually spans nearly 40 years of Janie's life, is "framed" by an evening visit between two friends.

The story that Janie tells is about love—how Janie sought love in four relationships. First, she looked for love from the grandmother who raised her. Next, she sought love from Logan Killicks, her first husband, a stodgy old potato farmer, who Nanny believed offered Janie security. Her third relationship involved Joe Starks. Their union lasted nearly 20 years and brought her economic security and an enviable position as the mayor's wife. Janie endured this marriage in the shadow of charismatic, ambitious Joe, a man who knew how to handle people, money, and power, but who had no perception of Janie's simple wish to be respected and loved.

Janie's final relationship was with migrant worker Tea Cake, who gave Janie the love that she had always desired. With Tea Cake, Janie was able to experience true love and happiness for the first time in her life. As a widow, Janie would sell Joe's crossroads store, close up her comfortable home, and leave with her new husband to share his life as a bean picker in the muck of the Everglades. Tea Cake introduced Janie to a new life in the Everglades. There she met new people, Tea Cake's fun-loving friends, and experienced another community. Her life with Tea Cake was far different than her life with Joe. This marriage and Janie's happiness lasted about 18 months—until a powerful hurricane devastated the land, and Tea Cake became a victim of it.

A few weeks after Tea Cake's death, Janie returns to Eatonville because she cannot bear to remain in the Everglades, where she is surrounded by memories of her beloved Tea Cake. She returns to her hometown, with her quest for sincere love having finally been fulfilled by Tea Cake. After an evening of retelling her past to her friend Pheoby, the story of Janie's life is complete.

List of Characters

Janie   Sixteen-year-old Janie Crawford dreams of love and wonders whether love will come with marriage. Twenty-four years and three marriages later, Janie has experienced both love and personal growth.

Nanny   Born into slavery on a plantation near Savannah, she bears Leafy, her white master's child. Disappointed with this child, Nanny, who has no given name, dotes on her granddaughter Janie.

Mrs. Washburn   Nanny's employer and benefactor.

Logan Killicks   Janie's first husband. He is an older man who can offer her protection and a 60-acre potato farm.

Joe Starks   The mayor of Eatonville and Janie's second husband. He is a proud, ambitious, self-centered man who has the power to get other people to do what he wants. The town of Eatonville is a monument to Joe Starks, and Janie is one of his prized possessions.

Vergible "Tea Cake" Woods   Fun-loving, guitar-playing, hardworking, Tea Cake is Janie's third husband and the fulfillment of her dreams of love.

Pheoby Watson   As Janie's best friend and confidante, Pheoby can be trusted to listen to Janie's story and tell the townsfolk as much or as little of it as she wishes. In either case, Janie knows that Pheoby will be honest. [**Note:** Hurston spells Pheoby's name in a most unusual way. Usually, the name is spelled P-h-o-e-b-y. When taking a test or writing a paper about this novel, be sure to double-check the spelling of this character's name.]

Sam Watson   Pheoby's husband and a loyal supporter of Janie. He has little patience with the porch sitters.

Mrs. Turner   A talkative, color- and class-conscious restaurant owner in the Everglades. Her bigotry contrasts with Janie's open heart and mind.

The Porch Sitters   A group of men and a few women who sit on the porches of their homes, as well as on the porch of Joe Starks' crossroads store, and diligently mind everyone else's business, especially Janie's. The women who gossip about Janie as she trudges into the town are Pearl Stone, Mrs. Sumpkins, and Lulu Moss. Some of the men have minor speaking roles in this story, but for the most part, they simply represent the community, Joe and Janie's town. Among them are Lee Coker, Guv'nor Amos Hicks, Tony Taylor, Lige Moss, Hambo, Pearson, Brother Davis (the preacher), Sim Jones, Oscar Scott, Jeff Bruce, Matt Bonner, Walter Thomas, and Sam Watson. Hezekiah Potts helps Janie in the store after Joe's death.

The Workers in the Muck These men and women are the community of migrant laborers in the bean fields of the Everglades; Janie accepts them because they are Tea Cake's friends and, therefore, hers. They spend their spare time having fun rather than porch sitting and gossiping. Most of them are identified by colorful nicknames: Ed Dockery, Sop-de-Bottom, Stew Beef, Coodemay, 'Lias, Bootnyny, Motor Boat, Sterrett, and Muck-Boy. Mrs. Turner and her husband are not farm workers.

Nunkie A young girl foolish enough to go after Tea Cake.

Character Map

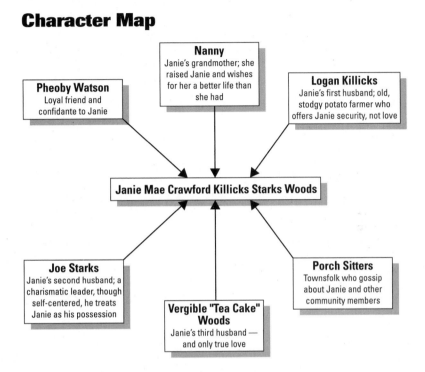

Nanny
Janie's grandmother; she raised Janie and wishes for her a better life than she had

Pheoby Watson
Loyal friend and confidante to Janie

Logan Killicks
Janie's first husband; old, stodgy potato farmer who offers Janie security, not love

Janie Mae Crawford Killicks Starks Woods

Joe Starks
Janie's second husband; a charismatic leader, though self-centered, he treats Janie as his possession

Vergible "Tea Cake" Woods
Janie's third husband — and only true love

Porch Sitters
Townsfolk who gossip about Janie and other community members

CRITICAL COMMENTARIES

Chapter 1

Summary

The porch sitters are spread out on the front porch of Pheoby and Sam Watson's home, happy to be free of the responsibilities of their long day's labor. They are astonished to see a bedraggled and weary-looking Janie Starks trudging into town, then turning her face in their direction. The women see her as a disaster, but the men see her as still possessing physical attraction. Janie speaks, acknowledges them, and goes on, and their indignation is great. How could she have the nerve not to stop and explain why she went off a year and a half ago in a blue satin dress and now she returns in dirty overalls?

Surely her husband—they assume she married the man, the guitar-playing, roving Tea Cake—took her money and probably went off with a younger woman. After all, Tea Cake was nearly ten years younger than Janie. They believe that Janie should have stopped and talked to them. The inherent jealousy of the women is quite apparent.

Janie's friend Pheoby defends her to the porch sitters. Pheoby believes that Janie does not have to share any of her personal business with them. Assuming that Janie is hungry, Pheoby volunteers to take Janie a pot of mulatto rice, and soon she finds her way through the darkness to Janie's back steps. Pheoby's motive is not completely unselfish. She is quietly certain that Janie will talk to her and explain what happened during the past year and a half. Janie welcomes her friend and the gift of food. She informs Pheoby that Tea Cake did not run off with the money that Joe left her. She reveals that the money is safe in the bank, but Tea Cake is dead. After Janie has rested for a while, cleaned and soothed her tired feet, and enjoyed the rice, she tells Pheoby about her months with Tea Cake.

Commentary

Their Eyes Were Watching God opens with a focus on judgment, a powerful and prevalent theme in the novel. As Janie returns to Eatonville after a lengthy absence, the porch sitters treat her especially harshly when talking about her. They make it their business to criticize her past actions and her present appearance, while ultimately judging her. This theme of judgment will continue throughout the novel, as Janie will be judged by her husbands and others.

Thus, the character of Janie Mae Crawford Killicks Starks Woods, the novel's 40-year-old heroine, is introduced as she endures the judgments of the porch sitters. Readers will come to know Janie as a strong, independent, free-spirited woman who strives to define herself, rather than allow others to determine who she is. In the novel, Janie encounters many people who attempt to define her by her beauty or by her relationships with others, just as the porch sitters do in the first chapter.

Besides Janie, Pheoby Watson is introduced as Janie's loyal confidante and best friend. In this chapter, Pheoby, who is genuine and kind, contrasts with the porch sitters, who are mean and superficial. Pheoby shows true care and concern for her friend as she offers Janie rice as well as a listening ear. While the character of Pheoby is minor in the novel, she represents true friendship for Janie.

The end of the chapter sets the format for the remainder of the novel. Janie tells Pheoby that she cannot tell her about her experiences without relating the events of her life. This first chapter takes place in the present, while the remaining chapters (until the last) are composed of Janie's recollections of her past.

Glossary

(Here and in the following chapters, difficult words and phrases, as well as allusions and historical references, are explained.)

porch sitters   hard-working farmers and laborers; men and women who work for someone else—a white boss. Only in the evening do they gain control of their time. Janie's late husband, Joe Starks, seems to be the only man in Eatonville who didn't work for someone else.

dat ole forty year ole 'oman   a reference to Janie; the remark, by a woman, about a woman, is made out of spite and envy. Although Janie is 40 years old, she is still an attractive woman, much to the annoyance of the women.

bander log   possibly a long log that people sat on while they bantered, joked, and gossiped.

fall to their level   The women hope that Janie will someday, somehow, stop having an aura about her. Her charisma reinforces their envy and is proof that they do not think well of themselves.

to study about   Mrs. Sumpkins' phrase that means she isn't "thinking about" Janie; ironically, from her remarks, she has evidently spent much time doing just that.

She sits high, but she looks low   Lulu Moss suggests that while Janie carries herself in a high-mannered way, her social standing has come down considerably after her relationship with Tea Cake.

booger man   the mythical monster who is often called the "boogeyman"; a frightening imaginary being, often used as a threat in disciplining children.

mulatto rice   a concoction of cooked rice, chopped and browned onions, crisp bacon bits, and some chopped tomatoes.

lamps and chimneys   the reference is to kerosene lamps. Apparently, Janie, a good housekeeper, either left the lamps clean when she went away or took time to clean at least one of them as soon as she returned. Kerosene lamps and their chimneys must be clean in order to function properly.

stove wood   Although Janie has the most pretentious house in town, it does not have gas or electricity; she must cook on a wood-burning stove.

Mouth-Almighty   someone who talks too much.

An envious heart makes the treacherous ear   Pheoby characterizes the gossipy women with this biblical-sounding adage.

a lost ball in de high grass   The townspeople love baseball; not only do they like to watch it, but they also like to play it. The field where they play has tall, uncut grass, and fly balls are often lost and the game delayed while both teams search for the ball.

They don't know if life is a mess of corn-meal dumplings and if love is a bed quilt   The experiences of the townspeople are so limited that they can't make any valid observations on life and love.

come kiss and be kissed   come and talk to me, Janie is saying; it's implied that the townspeople should do more of this in their lives.

The 'ssociation of life . . . De Grand Lodge, de big convention of livin'   Janie refers here to the common experience of belonging to fraternal or church organizations and going to their conventions and meetings. Janie wants Pheoby to understand that her experiences in the past eighteen months were as exciting as attending a convention.

hard of understandin'   Pheoby will want a detailed explanation to be sure that she understands all that Janie says.

a mink skin . . . a coon hide   one thing looks pretty much like something else until both can be studied carefully. No one can understand what Janie's life was like with Tea Cake or with Joe until each is examined carefully.

monstropolous   hyperbole invented by Hurston; perhaps an extension of monstrous.

Chapter 2

Summary

Janie begins the recollection of her life with an overview of her years with Nanny, her grandmother. She and Nanny lived in a house on the property of Mrs. Washburn, Nanny's very sympathetic and helpful white employer. Janie played with Mrs. Washburn's white grandchildren, and it was not until she saw herself in a group picture, when she was six years old, that she discovered that she was not white. As a child, she had happy times, but those times ended when the girls at school picked on her because she came to school better dressed and better groomed than they did; she even wore ribbons in her hair. They told Janie derogatory stories about her father and omitted anything positive. According to Janie, her father tried to get in touch with her mother with offers of marriage.

Nanny believed things would be better for Janie if they did not live with Mrs. Washburn. Nanny was a woman of ambition and determination. She accepted help from her employer and was thus able to purchase land and a small house with a yard that Janie loved.

One spring afternoon while Nanny is sleeping, Janie lingers in the yard under her favorite pear tree. Johnny Taylor, known to the neighbors and to Janie as lazy, passes by the fence and stops to talk to Janie— and kisses her. Nanny wakes in time to see the kiss and memories of her life and that of her daughter run through her mind. It is time now, the old lady knows, for Janie to have protection for herself in the form of a solid, respectable husband. The girl's life cannot be ruined by some trifling youth like Johnny Taylor.

Janie protests that the meeting was accidental and that the kiss was innocent, but Nanny is unconvinced. In an emotional scene, Nanny rocks and embraces Janie. When they are both calm, Nanny tells Janie how much she loves her. Now is the time for Nanny to tell Janie about her own life.

Although Nanny was born into slavery on a plantation near Savannah, Nanny had dreams. The fact that she was a slave would not allow her to do more than dream, but Emancipation gave her freedom and a chance to transfer those dreams to her daughter Leafy. Leafy, whose father was Nanny's white master, disappointed Nanny; one day she left home, leaving behind the infant Janie. Nanny now sees Janie as another chance for her to see her dreams fulfilled, and those dreams do not include Johnny Taylor.

Nanny had opportunities to marry, she tells Janie, but she chose not to, preferring to dedicate her life to her granddaughter. Now it is time for Janie to marry, and Nanny has chosen Logan Killicks, a much older man, who can offer Janie the protection and security of his age, plus a 60-acre potato farm.

Janie protests the plan, but Nanny knows that she can do no more for Janie. She has done her best. Someone else must now care for Janie.

Commentary

Chapter 2 serves as the exposition of the novel by providing valuable background information about the characters of Janie and Nanny. Readers learn for the first time about Janie's childhood, her absent mother, and Nanny's life as a slave on a southern plantation. Readers now can understand Nanny's sincere need to protect Janie from the evils of the world. She wants Janie to have a better, more secure life than she (and her daughter) did.

Literary
Device

For the first time in the novel, Hurston compares Janie's life to a tree with the simile, "Janie saw her life like a great tree in leaf with the things suffered, things enjoyed, things done, and undone." The image of the tree continues as Janie becomes infatuated with a blossoming pear tree in Nanny's backyard. While the first image compared Janie's life to a tree, this next image causes Janie to make a realization. As she watches a bee enter the center of a bloom to extract pollen, Janie suddenly understands what she believes to be the concepts of love and marriage. Although Janie is married three times in the novel, it is not until her third marriage that she encounters true love. It becomes evident that, more than anything, Janie yearns for true, unconditional love. Hurston's tree image appears again as she uses the metaphor, "She had glossy leaves and bursting buds and she wanted to struggle with life but it seemed to elude her." At 16, Janie yearns for the answers to life's questions, especially those queries about love.

The narrative shifts in chapter 2 as Janie's history is revealed. As Hurston begins the description of the blossoming pear tree, the point of view shifts from Janie's voice to a third-person narrator who tells a story about Janie, rather than a story told by Janie.

A new character is also introduced in Chapter 2. Janie's grandmother has chosen Logan Killicks, a much older man, to be Janie's husband. Nanny believes Logan to be the perfect choice for Janie because he offers her protection as well as stability because he owns a 60-acre potato farm. Janie protests her grandmother's plan because she does not know Logan, let alone love him. Janie's images of perfect love emanate from the pear tree, and according to Janie, "The vision of Logan Killicks was desecrating the tree. . . ." Janie's brief marriage to Logan failed to bring her the happiness, love, and acceptance that she desired.

Note that in this chapter, Janie calls herself "a real dark little girl." Later on in this novel, she is described as having skin like coffee and cream. Hurston is not always consistent, but such discrepancies do not alter the powerful narrative of the story.

Glossary

never hit us a lick amiss   never beat or spanked the children when they didn't deserve it.

palma christi leaves   the leaves of a gigantic herb plant called *palma christi* in Spanish-speaking countries; its leaves are believed to reduce severe headaches.

bore the burden in the heat of the day   The biblical reference is to Matthew 20:12: "These latecomers did only one hour's work, yet you have treated them on a level with us, who have sweated the whole day long in the blazing sun."

school out . . . high bush and sweeter berry   take more time to look around and think about what you want to do. Picking a good husband is compared to knowing what part of a berry bush has the sweetest fruit.

angel with the sword   a metaphor for death; the biblical reference comes from Numbers 22:23: ". . . the angel standing in the door with his sword drawn. . . ."

got in quotation wid people   Sherman's march had ended, the slaves had been freed, and the Union had set up a system to help the freedmen. It was only by talking around, though, that Nanny found out what was going on.

Chapter 3

Summary

Nanny's friends attend Janie's wedding, which is held in Nanny's parlor on a Saturday evening. The guests are generously served three cakes and such hearty delicacies as fried rabbit and chicken. As always, Mrs. Washburn helps with the affair. Janie gets a good send-off into marriage, and she and her new husband ride away in Logan's wagon to his lonely home. The farm apparently is adjacent to the road, but the house is set back, almost in the woods, and for Janie, it is a dreary place.

After three months' time, Janie comes to visit Nanny at Mrs. Washburn's, arriving just as Nanny is making some beaten biscuits. Love has not come into Janie's marriage as she thought it would. She had convinced herself before the wedding that husbands and wives come to love each other, but it is not happening. Nanny can't give the young bride the advice she seeks. Instead, almost prophetically, Nanny admonishes Janie that she is still young, and many things can happen in her life. This wait-and-see advice, however, is not what Janie came to hear, and so she returns home. Within a month, Nanny is dead.

Commentary

Janie hopes that her marriage to Logan Killicks will bring her love and happiness. As she says to her grandmother, "Ah wants to want him sometimes." Janie's and Nanny's views of marriage clearly contrast with one another. Nanny wishes Janie a comfortable, secure life, unlike what she had. However, Janie yearns for a marriage filled with unconditional love. While Nanny's wishes for Janie's marriage were filled with good intent, this marriage only brought Janie feelings of unhappiness and loneliness.

Although she protested the marriage, Janie hopes her relationship with Logan will blossom and their love for each other will grow. As she says, "Ah wants things sweet wid mah marriage lak when you sit under a pear tree and think." After two and a half months, however, Janie still feels lonely in her marriage, just as she does in Logan's home, a place she describes as "a lonesome place like a stump in the middle of the woods where nobody had ever been."

Character Insight

By the close of this chapter, Janie's hopes for love and for her marriage are dashed and she feels more alone than she ever has before. In this chapter, Janie comes to a powerful realization about love and marriage. She now understands that "marriage did not make love." At this point, Janie's dream of love and happiness dies, causing her to leave the naïve young girl that she was when she married Logan and to become a woman.

Glossary

beaten biscuits   Southern cooks have long prided themselves on their beaten biscuits, pounding the dough for 20 or 30 minutes with a mallet or hammer, beating air into it until it is light.

knocked up   pregnant.

kissin' yo' foot   acting more like a servant than a husband and an equal.

buy and sell such as them   Nanny is concerned about both the protection and economic security that Logan can offer Janie.

Chapter 4

Summary

The marriage is still in its first year when Logan reassesses his bride. Work on his profitable farm is hard, and he needs help in the fields. His first wife, he points out to Janie, worked hard—plowed and chopped wood—and he expects the same from Janie. Logan remarks that Janie has been spoiled both by her grandmother and him.

One day, Logan gives Janie the task of cutting seed potatoes while he drives the mule over to Lake City to inquire about buying a second mule, a gentle animal that Janie can use to plow. Janie settles down in a pleasant spot in the yard to do her potato work. She can see the road from where she is sitting, and soon Joe Starks comes down the road and greets her. She gives him some refreshing well water, and they talk. In introducing himself, he says that he hails from Georgia. She tells him enough about herself for him to know that she does not belong on a backwoods potato farm. He teases her about being so young and scorns the idea of her being behind a plow. Joe goes on his way, and Janie returns to her chore, dreaming of love and a less strenuous life.

Joe and Janie meet every day after that, and one night, Janie has a talk with Logan and suggests that she might run off and leave him. Although he is deeply hurt, he laughs at the idea and tells her that if she did, she would soon be back. Early the next day, Logan asserts his power over Janie by demanding that she leave her work in the kitchen to help him move a manure pile. Janie refuses, and they argue. The fact that Janie has not been raised to do farm work or hire out as a domestic irritates him. He accuses her of degrading him—honest and hardworking man that he is. Logan, the tough, old farmer, is almost reduced to tears, but Janie is adamant. Furthermore, Janie now has a means of escape because she and Joe have plans to meet.

Janie returns to the kitchen to finish some breakfast preparations, then leaves the farm. Joe is waiting for her, and they ride off in a hired rig, headed toward Green Cove Springs, where they will be married.

Commentary

Chapter 4 serves to show the decline of Janie and Logan's marriage. After a year of marriage, Logan begins to reevaluate Janie's role as his wife. He desires a wife who is hardworking. Logan lacks respect for Janie, and he treats her almost like a slave, requiring her to complete mundane tasks. Logan believes Janie has been spoiled both by her grandmother and by him. When Logan confronts Janie, he compares her to his first wife, who chopped wood for him without making any complaints.

For the first time, Janie becomes feisty with Logan, saying "If you can stand not to chop wood and tote wood Ah reckon you can stand not to git no dinner." She stands up to Logan again when she tells him, "You ain't done me no favor by marryin' me. And if dat's what you call yo'self doin, Ah don't thank yuh for it." This is not the life that Janie had hoped for, but her luck changes when she hears a man whistling as he walks down the road.

Character Insight

Joe Starks, a stylish, sophisticated man from Georgia, is introduced in this chapter. Joe serves as a sharp contrast to Logan. He tells Janie that she has no business working in the fields. He believes, rather, that she should be relaxing and enjoying life. He says, "A pretty doll-baby lak you is made to sit on de front porch and rock and fan yo'self and eat p'taters dat other folks plant just special for you." Janie likes Joe because "he spoke for change and chance." For Janie, Joe represents something new—a "far horizon." This becomes Janie's new journey. She desires to experience what the world has to offer, and Joe can assist her on this journey. As Janie leaves, she knows "The change was bound to do her good." In reference to the pear tree metaphor, Joe serves as the "bee" for Janie's "bloom."

Glossary

freezolity   indifference, or a lack of interest.

sleeveholders   fancy elastic bands similar to women's garters, worn on the upper arm of a shirt sleeve to be sure that the cuff falls exactly where the wearer wants it.

in and through Georgy   living in and passing through the state of Georgia.

sugar-tit   cloth tied around a bit of sugar to form a nipple-like pacifier for a baby.

ribbon-cane syrup   sorghum molasses.

fall down and wash up   fall down and worship.

yo' royal diasticutis   a sarcastic reference to Janie's buttocks.

Chapter 5

Summary

Married life with Joe Starks seems to get off to a good start as Janie and her husband ride the train to the new town ("...a town all outa colored folks...") that he told her about. He indulges her by buying little trinkets, and she is impressed by his ability to talk to strangers. While she studies him and compares his rather portly figure to those of white folks, Joe talks about his plans for the town where they will live.

When they arrive in town, both are disappointed. It is much less than either of them expected, yet Joe is undaunted. He is full of ideas, and he has the money and the energy to carry them out. Having assessed the unprogressive nature of the town, Joe first arranges for a place for them to live, and next, sets a date for a town meeting to form a committee. The local men are impressed by Joe's overwhelming personality and Janie's good looks.

Joe rents a house for a month, and he and his wife settle in. The men gather around, and Joe picks them for information. They tell him that the town has a choice of two names: West Maitland or Eatonville. It will become Eatonville in honor of Captain Eaton, one of the original land donors.

Fifty acres is not enough land for a town, Joe decides, and, much to the amazement of the townsmen, he goes off to buy more land. Their skepticism is immense, but so is Joe's self-confidence. He returns with the papers for 200 acres. While he is away, one of the local men tries to work up a conversation with Janie, yet she coolly rebuffs him.

Joe moves fast to build a crossroads store and to secure a government post office for the town. He begins selling off portions of his 200 acres to new settlers, the town grows rapidly, and when Joe's new store is completed, he holds a party. The men who will become the porch sitters preside over the party, teasing and joking with one another. Joe makes a speech, but he refuses to let Janie say anything. He comes away from the meeting with what he wants: the position of elected mayor.

So far, this has been Joe's Eatonville, and now that the store and post office are functioning, Joe announces to Janie that she must work in the store, because he is simply too busy. Janie demurs because the street is dark, but Joe has an answer for that. He writes Sears, Roebuck, and Company, pays for a street light, and has a big barbecue festival after the lamp has been installed. Of course, it is Joe who climbs the ladder to be the first person to light the street lamp.

The long dark hair that was beribboned for the schoolgirl Janie becomes an item of jealousy for Joe. He makes Janie hide her hair under headrags while she works in the store because he is afraid that some other man might touch it or admire it. By now, Janie knows that she has no power to dispute Joe, and so she complies.

The women in the town have no way of knowing how unhappy their mayor's wife is. As they watch Joe push their men to upgrade the town, and as he builds an impressive house, their envy of Janie increases. Her feelings of being different, of being avoided, of not fitting in—those feelings she had as a schoolgirl—are repeated. As the mayor's wife, a woman certainly more prosperous than the other women, she realizes she can't get close to them for friendship. One friendship does develop, however, with Pheoby Watson.

The porch sitters soon take their places at Joe's and also observe and comment on the mayor's wife. They can't help but notice Joe's verbal abuse of her and her subservience to his harsh criticism of the mistakes she makes in the store and post office. They wonder about the quality of their marriage relationship.

Commentary

Joe has a powerful presence in Eatonville, and Janie finds herself in the background, dominated by her husband and his ambitions. Joe is infatuated with making Eatonville into a working city. The townspeople both respect and fear Joe. While they are grateful for the positive changes that he has brought to the town, they fear the power that he holds over them. Not only does Joe dominate Janie, he also commands the townspeople.

In his rise to power, Janie becomes Joe's possession, similar to the businesses and people of the town. For example, after Joe is appointed mayor, one of the townspeople, Tony, introduces Janie to make a speech. Before she even has a chance to speak, Joe interrupts explaining "mah wife don't know nothin' 'bout no speech-makin' . . . She's uh woman and her place is in de home." He craves the power that he has as mayor and he also uses it in his relationship with Janie. He fails to treat Janie as an equal, but rather as one of his town subjects. Joe also refuses to allow Janie to wear her long hair down for fear that other men might touch it. Joe fears that another man will charm his wife and snatch her away from him, just as he did when she was married to Logan. Janie abides by Joe's rules because she has no power to challenge him.

Character Insight

Joe's position as mayor causes Janie to feel cold, isolated, and lonely. Janie feels isolated from most of the townspeople. Besides Pheoby Watson, she has no other close friends. As the mayor's wife, many people keep their distance from Janie because "she slept with authority and so she was part of it in the town mind." Not only does Janie feel isolated from the townspeople, but also she feels isolated from her husband. She explains to Joe that his position as mayor exerts a "strain" on their relationship. Joe believes Janie should be grateful to him for making "uh big woman" out of her. No longer is Janie an individual; she is the mayor's wife. For the second time, marriage for Janie is not what she had hoped.

Glossary

sitting on their shoulder blades a position that's closer to lying down that sitting.

a huge live oak tree an evergreen oak.

uh mite too previous In this particular colloquialism, "previous" means "a little too early."

Middle Georgy the middle of the state of Georgia.

Ah'm uh son of Combunction a polite way of swearing; similar to "Well, I'll be a son of a gun. . . ."

All de women in de world ain't . . . teppentine still and saw mill camp free and easy women, women from the lowest level of laborers. Turpentine stills and saw mills were usually located in the woods, removed from town and close to the trees essential for their products.

Isaac and Rebecca at de well   This biblical reference is not literally accurate. Isaac never met Rebecca at the well. Isaac's father's servant encountered Rebecca at the well. The servant had prayed for divine guidance in finding a wife for Isaac—that after his long journey to the land of Aramnaharaim, a generous and humble woman would approach him at the community well and offer him a drink of fresh water from her jug, as well as to offer to draw sufficient water for his camels. Rebecca did so and agreed to leave her village and travel to the land of Canaan to become Isaac's wife.

All them dat's goin' tuh cut de monkey   in other words, if everyone has finished acting silly.

bell-cow   the leader of the herd; here, the most important women in town.

Protolapsis uh de cutinary linin'   The reference is to something that upsets the stomach and makes a person nervous. Hurston is pointing out the men's fondness for impressive words, whether they have real meaning or not.

the street lamp   Before electric lights were common, cities and towns lighted their streets with gas lamps. The lamplighter would go around at dusk with a small four- or five-step ladder which he would climb to open the globe of the lamp and light the wick.

Chapter 6

Summary

The porch sitters soon take up daily residence on the porch of Joe's store. There, they delight in accusing dimwitted Matt Bonner of mistreating his yellow mule. Matt and his mule become a favorite topic of conversation and teasing, and the porch sitters vie with one another in tantalizing Matt, accusing him of overworking and nearly starving the animal. Janie listens to the talk and is amused by it. She has in mind some comical stories she'd like to tell, but Joe forbids her to take part in the chatter. He calls the people trashy, unworthy of conversation with the mayor's wife.

One afternoon, the men engage in a game of mule-baiting. In a natural defensive reaction, the mule fights back, but the more the animal resists, the more the men tease him. Finally, Janie mutters her disapproval, which Joe overhears. In a surprising act of kindness, both for the mule and for Janie, he purchases the animal. From then on, it becomes the town pet, living in the front yard of the store and rambling about at will, leading a life of ease and freedom. Joe has done an act of unselfishness for Janie.

The mule finally dies of old age, and the townspeople stage an elaborate mock funeral service before they leave the carcass to buzzards. Joe joins in the hilarious parody, but Janie does what Joe tells her to do: She stays in the store. When Joe returns, still chuckling at the foolishness, they briefly discuss the role of fun and play in the serious business of survival and daily living.

One day, Joe discovers that a bill of shipment has been misplaced and a desired item is not in stock. He berates Janie severely, and she tries to answer with comments about his own deficiencies. As usual, Joe prevails, and Janie gives up trying to defend herself. Thus, Joe is satisfied with her apparent submission.

On a day when everything goes wrong in the kitchen, Joe slaps Janie. At this moment, Janie knows beyond any doubt and hope that this marriage will never be what she wants. All she can do is summon the courage to put on a good face and endure it.

Joe goes through the motions of being kind to a customer, perhaps because he can't be kind to Janie. He helps Mrs. Tony, a town parasite and slovenly housekeeper, get some groceries for her family. The porch sitters observe the scene and remark that the woman's husband loves her and puts up with her faults, an observation lost on Joe.

Commentary

Mock arguments on pseudo-serious subjects, such as those about the mule, found in this chapter often occupy the porch sitters as they struggle to understand their position in the world. They also serve as a form of entertainment for the porch sitters. These discussions do not involve Janie, Joe, or even the town of Eatonville, but they help characterize the men and provide an interlude of local color.

Joe's domination over Janie continues. As the porch sitters share gossip and conversation, Janie longs to take part in this idle chatter, but Joe forbids her to associate with such "trashy people." As a result of his jealousy, he continues to forbid Janie from showing her hair in the store. Joe feels threatened that another man might steal Janie, his possession, away from him. (Perhaps Joe feels even more vulnerable because he actually stole Janie from Logan Killicks.) Joe believes that "she was there in the store for *him* to look at, not the others." Janie, like the majority of the town is a possession, owned by Joe.

In this chapter, much of the conversation among the porch sitters centers on Matt Bonner's helpless mule. When the men torture the animal, the mule fights, but the men only tease him more. The mule serves to symbolize Janie and her struggle with Joe. Just as the mule has been starved from food, Janie has been denied love and affection from Joe. Joe demands Janie's complete compliance and he continues to dominate her.

Janie finally realizes that her marriage to Joe is a sham, but she also realizes that she has no way out. When Joe slaps Janie one day after his dinner fails to meet his expectations, Janie's "image of [Joe] tumbled down and shattered." Janie knows now more than ever that she must endure her husband and his abuse.

In this chapter, Janie speaks out against the torturing of the mule. She believes that "people ought to have some regard for helpless things." Like the mule, Janie, too, feels helpless in her marriage to Joe. Each time that Janie attempts to stand up to her husband, he only makes her life more difficult by ridiculing or hurting her. Joe has suppressed her so many times that she has stopped speaking her mind. Joe holds all of the power, and Janie has none.

Literary Device

The use of irony is also evident in Chapter 6. Near the end of the chapter, Joe treats Mrs. Tony with sympathy and kindness, even though he cannot be compassionate to his own wife. Perhaps Joe treats Mrs. Tony with compassion because the townspeople are present to witness his act of kindness. With Janie, Joe has no audience, and so he feels no need to pretend.

Glossary

... and yo' feet ain't mates In the first part of Matt's response, he does something that frequently occurs in folk speech: He equates the man Sam with a lie. "You'se a lie, Sam," he says, adding "Yo' feet ain't mates," meaning that Sam is not put together right and hence can't be believed.

Feeds 'im offa 'come up' and seasons it wid raw-hide This is a way of saying that the animal is not well fed. "Come up" would be a promise—someone is waiting for something to come up, a job, for example. Rawhide is untanned cattle skin, certainly not very palatable for man or beast. Rawhide is also a material used for whips.

rub board The old-fashioned galvanized or glass washing board was in common use before washing machines became economically available.

before de ornery varmit could tack a sailing and boating term, consistent with the strong wind that was blowing during this episode. To a sailor, "tack" means to turn the bow to the wind. The mule wasn't fast enough to turn and run into the wind in pursuit of the children.

Say you started tuh Miccanopy but de mule ... Miccanopy is a small community northwest of Eatonville. The man didn't really know where he was going.

Folks up dat way don't eat biscuit bread but once a week Biscuits must be made of white wheat flour, something better than corn-meal. Cornmeal is the staple of the poor, used in corn bread, corn pone, hush puppies, cornmeal mush, and a host of other stomach-filling items. Biscuits are special and an indication of some prosperity.

side-meat   Matt bought side meat by the slice. Side meat is meat from the side of a pig, specifically bacon or salt pork. In Joe's store, it would be sold by the slab to be sliced at home by the purchaser or sliced and weighed in the store. This is another indication of Matt's poverty or ignorance—or both.

fractious   hard to manage; unruly; rebellious; also, peevish; irritable; cross.

goosing   a sudden, playful prod in the backside.

black gaiters   ankle-high shoes with elastic gores at the sides. For Joe, they would be a classy sort of houseslipper.

crazy as a betsy bug   a variation of "crazy as a bed bug," an insect of a family (Cimicidae) of wingless, bloodsucking hemipteran insects, especially the species (*Cimex lectularius*) with a broad, flat reddish-brown body and an unpleasant odor that infests beds, furniture, walls, and so on, is active mainly at night, and may transmit a variety of diseases.

you didn't have gumption   "Gumption" is shrewdness in practical matters; common sense.

Drag him out to the edge of the hammock   a precarious place to be because a hammock tips very easily when the occupant gets too close to the edge.

No Matt Bonner with plow lines   Plow lines control an animal. Now that the mule is dead, he will no longer be hitched to the plow.

Ah knowed you would going tuh crawl up dat holler   In other words, I knew that you were going to take that path in the discussion. Sam will "smoke out" Lige in his rebuttal. The two men engage in regular and predictable arguments. Each one knows pretty well what the other one will say, but all of this is part of the entertainment on the porch of the store.

uh butt-headed cow   a stubborn animal that won't do what its owner wants it to do.

dat great big ole scoundrel beast up dere   The speaker is referring to a picture of an enormous dinosaur on a billboard advertising the Sinclair Oil Company. A dinosaur was the logo of Sinclair and was prominently displayed at their filling stations. In all likelihood, the men do not know it is a dinosaur.

Daisy is walking a drum tune   The drum is the key percussion instrument in a musical group. It sets the tempo. Daisy is walking with the stylish snap of a precision solo drummer—and she knows it!

a "studied jury"   Educational resources were limited for this community, and there were very few men with college degrees in law or medicine—or even the ministry. In *Mules and Men*, Hurston has a character say, "You see when Ah was studyin' doctor . . ." Whereas a man or woman might get a "call" to the ministry, the path to informal law or medicine was self-study or perhaps apprenticeship with a practitioner.

Sam Watson, you'se mah fish   a good catch—not an empty hook for the fisherman or woman. Joe plans to beat Sam at checkers— that is catch him like a fish on his hook.

Chapter 7

Summary

The long years of the empty, loveless marriage go on. Janie develops an outward appearance of compliance, but inwardly she is saving her emotions. Seventeen years pass, and Joe, more than Janie, begins visibly aging. His vanity makes it hard for him to accept his aging and his as-yet-unadmitted illness. Characteristically, he transfers his frustration about his decline to Janie; one day he even orders her away from a croquet game because he says it's something for young folks.

Joe shows signs of physical decline: an aching back, increasing thinness, and grumpiness. His verbal abuse of Janie becomes worse, and the townfolks see that it has gone far beyond that to which they have been accustomed. Throughout the marriage, Joe never hesitates to insult Janie before them, and she always bites her tongue and accepts it, but as Joe's aging and illness make him even more bitter, Janie unexpectedly strikes back. Before an audience of porch sitters, she insults his manhood. This is Janie's emancipation, and Joe retaliates by striking her as hard as he can and making her leave the store.

Commentary

Chapter 7 serves as a pivotal point for Janie and her marriage. As the years have passed, Janie has become totally submissive to Joe, to avoid both his physical and verbal abuse. Joe has made an effort over the years to ridicule Janie even more when there was an audience to witness his cruelty. However, when Janie makes a mistake while cutting chewing tobacco, Joe lashes out at Janie in the middle of the store by criticizing her intelligence and her beauty.

Style & Language

Suddenly, something changes for Janie. She says that she felt as if "somebody snatched off part of a woman's clothes while she wasn't looking and the street were crowded." After years of his oppression, Janie stands up for herself before Joe and a group of townspeople. She begins to take control of her life, by telling Joe what she really thinks. By lashing out, she "had robbed him of his illusion of irresistible maleness that all men cherish, which was terrible."

Joe's destruction heightens, causing both Janie and himself great emotional pain. Janie has exposed Joe before the townspeople, causing him great embarrassment. Not only has Janie spoken out against Joe, but also the townspeople laughed, "cast[ing] down his empty armor before men." To show that he still holds power over Janie, Joe responds by striking Janie as hard as he possibly can. Smacking Janie is his only means of saving face. It is apparent that Joe is losing control over his own life, with his declining health and the disobedience of his wife.

Glossary

Then too she considered thirty-five is twice seventeen Janie has grown older and is more experienced than when Nanny married her off to Logan Killicks. She realizes how much of her life has passed. Accurate addition isn't important, the passage of time is.

Y'all really playin' de dozens tuhnight trading insults, usually in a predictable way, but the insults are based on exaggeration of personal traits and involve derogatory statements about members of each other's family—often, someone's mother.

The thing that Saul's daughter had done to David In I Samuel 18–19, Saul has two daughters, Merab and Michal. Saul gave Michal to David, and she saved his life. Saul was immensely jealous of David because of his youth, beauty, intelligence, and potential power. Saul wanted to kill him, but Michal foiled the plot.

Chapter 8

Summary

Joe and Janie's meaningless marriage is now shattered. Joe moves out of their bedroom, and as his illness progresses, he refuses to let Janie take care of him. He also stubbornly refuses to see a medical doctor, preferring instead to seek cures from quacks and charlatans. Janie, who doesn't want to give up the custodial responsibilities of a wife, finally gets a doctor, but it's too late. Joe's kidneys have failed, and he is a doomed man.

Although Joe has barred her from his sickroom, Janie goes to his bedside and tells the dying man some of the things that should have been said a long time ago. Joe is terrified at the thought of his impending death. In spite of the sincerity of Janie's pleas that he should realize their marriage did not bring them the happiness they both desired when they took that train to Eatonville, Joe dies unrepentant, and Janie looks on with pity for her dead husband.

Commentary

Even as Joe is dying, he still tries to exert his control over Janie. He bans her from his sickroom and refuses to allow Janie to care for him. Joe does not desire Janie's pity; he wants Janie to feel guilty for standing up to him in front of the townspeople even though it was years ago. Janie, however, will not allow Joe to manipulate her even as he is dying.

Again, Janie stands up to Joe. After entering Joe's room, she refuses to leave, even when he demands that she do so. Janie insists that the man she ran away with 20 years ago is gone, and Joe is "whut's left after he died."

Joe has never been able to accept Janie for who she truly is. His refusal has been the basis for their marital troubles. Joe forbid Janie to speak for herself and to be her own person. He wanted Janie to be the woman that he wanted her to be. For several years, Janie kept her feelings to herself and obeyed Joe. On two occasions, in the store and as Joe is dying, she exerts her independence by standing up for herself.

Literary Device

Also in Chapter 8, Hurston employs a metaphor for death. Death, according to Janie, is "a strange being" with a sword "waiting for the messenger to bid him come." Hurston uses this powerful metaphor to show that Joe feared death and would only die when "the icy sword of the square-toed one had cut off his breath and left his hands in a pose of antagonizing protest."

Glossary

Well, if she must eat out of a long-handled spoon, she must A long-handled spoon has a long history in the English language. Chaucer uses it in *The Squire's Tale*: "Therfore bihooeth hire ful loong spoon/That shal ete with a feend." It also occurs in Shakespeare's *Comedy of Errors*: "He must have a long spoon that must eat with the devil." Joe has become almost evil in his illness, and Janie must treat him with all caution—with a long-handled spoon, something that she would use if she were to dine with the devil. References to a long-handled spoon are treated in most standard books of quotations.

de big fuss in de store dat Joe was 'fixed' and you wuz de one dat did it Here again, the busybodies are at work, suggesting that Janie has put some sort of spell on Joe. Joe is terminally ill, and the people do not understand the illness. It is much easier for them to accuse Janie of putting a voodoo spell on Joe to hasten his death than it is for them to understand that Joe's condition is helpless.

Ah been feelin' dat somethin' set for still-bait In other words, she is saying that she's feeling like she's the target of the community disapproval, like a bait on a hook that can't move or wriggle as a worm might do.

Last summer dat multiplied cock-roach wuz round heah tryin' tuh sell gophers Janie and Pheoby have no time for the charlatan, the "two-headed" doctor, the scheming, self-serving quack. Note the hyperbole "multiplied cock-roach." Note also that "gopher" could be a mispronunciation of "goopher," a well-known conjure mixture. It is usually an herb-root mixture alleged to have great power to do whatever the two-headed doctor said it would do.

He'd be all right just as soon as the two-headed man found what had been buried against him   Hurston discusses this phrase of conjure in *Mules and Men*. If indeed Janie has "fixed" Joe, then the conjure man has to find out what the "fix" is and where it is buried. His next task would be to concoct something that would counteract the "fix." All of this was done for a fee, of course, preferably paid in advance.

Chapter 9

Summary

Janie spares no expense for Joe's funeral. Even people from neighboring towns attend his funeral. She does what is expected of her as a widow, but she hides her true feelings behind the required mourning attire. Inwardly, Janie feels no sorrow.

Janie's first act of freedom is to burn all of the headrags that Joe made her wear. Aside from that, she makes no changes. She keeps the store with the help of a teenage youth, Hezekiah, who does his best to emulate Joe's mannerisms, even down to his cigar. Now Janie can sit on the porch and talk if she chooses.

What should she do? Seek her long-lost mother, Leafy? Go back to her hometown and tend to Nanny's grave? An undertaker of a nearby town is courting Janie, and moreover, suddenly men who were scarcely interested in her and Joe are now driving distances to inquire about her. For Janie, the best course is to enjoy her freedom and make the most of being alive.

Commentary

Style & Language

The funeral for the mule in Chapter 6 is a parody of every funeral and burial in which the townspeople of Eatonville have even been involved. In contrast, Joe's funeral may well be the most elaborate that they have ever seen. Janie spared no expense to make sure that Joe left "as he had come—with the out-stretched hand of power."

Janie's outward appearance and her inward thoughts contrast following the death of Joe. While the townspeople mourn the death of Joe, Janie appears to be grieving. However, inwardly, Janie feels no sorrow, only a sense of calm. Janie attended Joe's funeral, but inside, she "went rollicking with the springtime across the world." Finally, Janie is free of the man who stifled her individuality. In her first act of freedom following Joe's death, Janie burns her headrags to symbolize her new independence from Joe's control.

While many women who lose their husbands feel weak and insecure, Janie does not. Rather, Janie actually gains strength from Joe's death. Even though Janie endures intense loneliness, she is strong enough to manage her personal life and the store as a result of enduring Joe's constant ridicule. Ironically, Joe's domination may have made Janie a stronger person. Janie begins to enjoy her freedom: ". . . she liked being lonesome for a change. This freedom feeling was fine." One other positive outcome of Joe's death is Janie's deepening friendship with Pheoby. No longer is Janie restricted from maintaining friendships and socializing with the townspeople. With Joe's death, Janie has gained the freedom she has desired for so long.

Glossary

gold and red and purple, the gloat and glamor of secret orders Joe evidently belonged to several lodges or fraternal orders, and each one has a different ritual to be performed when a member dies. Hurston mentions the Elks (BPOE) band that plays at Joe's funeral.

celebration funerals and wakes often become festive affairs when family and friends gather, not only for the burial but also for a celebration of the life of the deceased.

set for still bait a term for fishing, meaning that the bait is easy for the fish to grab.

like a pack of chessy cats The reference is to the Cheshire Cat in *Alice in Wonderland,* who had an all-knowing smile. Here, Janie is saying that all of her gentlemen callers have smug, too-confident grins on their faces.

Chapter 10

Summary

Just about everyone in town has gone to a baseball game when Mr. Vergible Woods, better known as Tea Cake, arrives at Janie's store. He discovers that he has come to the wrong town for the baseball game, but he stays to visit with Janie. He is a tall, smiling, happy young man who quickly makes Janie laugh. He invites her to play checkers and is astounded when she tells him that she doesn't know the game. He teaches her how to play. Then, Tea Cake walks Janie home.

Commentary

The character of Vergible Woods, also known as Tea Cake, is introduced in Chapter 10. Tea Cake is a happy and attractive man, although he is 12 years younger than Janie. She is instantly attracted to his "full, lazy eyes, with the lashes curling sharply away like drawn scimitars. The lean, over-padded shoulders and narrow waist." With Tea Cake's arrival, Janie's loneliness seems to disappear, and she enjoys herself for the first time in a long time. Even after only visiting with Tea Cake for a short period of time, Janie feels like she has known Tea Cake all of her life.

Tea Cake brings excitement and new experiences to Janie's life, starting with the game of checkers. Joe forbid Janie to play the game with him or with other men, probably because that was another way he could exert his power and control over Janie. In addition, Joe would not want Janie to associate with the men of the town, since he would consider them a threat to his marriage with Janie. For Janie, this meeting with Tea Cake is truly just the beginning of her personal freedom and the new experiences that Tea Cake will offer her.

Glossary

kitchen matches These were a type of common household matches made for years by, among others, the Ohio Match Company. They were about two-and-a-half to three inches long and were sold in a box, the side of which contained a strip of abrasive-like fine sandpaper. The abrasive contained the chemicals needed to ignite the match when it was briskly scraped across the surface. Before electric stoves and gas stoves with the automatic pilot lights, no kitchen was complete without a box of these matches. Many campers still include them in their equipment.

cold-cocked her a look   looked her straight in the eyes.

Dixie Highway   U.S. Highway 1, the major Maine-to-Florida highway in the old U.S. highway system.

Ah done cut a hawg   I've made a mistake. Tea Cake thinks that perhaps he has said something he shouldn't have said.

Chapter 11

Summary

When Tea Cake visits, he is always welcome. He helps Janie in the store by frying fish, making corn bread, and entertaining customers by playing the guitar. One evening while Janie is relaxing, he begins combing her hair. He urges her to look at herself in the mirror, where she will see a reflection of a very attractive woman.

The two avoid one another at first. Janie is unsure that she can trust him, and Tea Cake is afraid that he will lose her. After a serious discussion about the age difference between them, he leaves, and Janie spends the next day thinking about him and trying to get him out of her mind. She finally accepts his intentions, and their relationship is consummated. Tea Cake then disappears for four days, and this causes Janie great anguish. When he returns, Tea Cake informs Janie that he has been working to make enough money to take her to the Sunday School picnic. Janie is concerned that Tea Cake is only inviting her to be polite. Tea Cake assures Janie that she is the only one for him.

Commentary

Style & Language

As a result of her two unhappy marriages, Janie is reluctant to build a relationship with Tea Cake, especially since Janie is considerably older than Tea Cake. However, Tea Cake encourages Janie to enjoy life and realize her beauty. Again, Hurston uses the images of bees, blossoms, and trees. This time, however, Tea Cake serves as the basis for the comparison. Janie reveals that "he could be a bee to a blossom—a pear tree blossom in the spring." Neither Logan nor Joe was compared using the metaphor. For the first time in the novel, Janie has found the love she has craved since she was a teenager.

Unlike both her previous husbands, Tea Cake does not judge Janie. The porch sitters, Logan, and Joe have judged Janie on her beauty, her work ethic, and her pursuit for her own identity. Tea Cake loves Janie unconditionally. He tells Janie that "nobody else on earth kin hold uh candle tuh you, baby." With Tea Cake, Janie can finally be herself.

One of Janie's most striking attributes is her long braids of hair. Joe exerted his power and control over Janie by demanding that she hide her braids under a head rag. Since Janie's braids served as a symbol of her beauty, Joe wanted her to conceal them so that other men might be discouraged from soliciting her. The image of Tea Cake combing Janie's hair serves to represent Janie's new found independence from Joe. Finally, she is free of Joe's control, which stifled her individuality and her beauty.

Glossary

You got me in de go long   opening for a proposal of marriage. Janie has captivated Tea Cake, and he will "go long" through life with her.

run our conversation from grassroots to pine trees   We've gone as far as we can go with this conversation—from minor matters to larger issues. Hurston has used other expressions like this to indicate limits and extremes in conversations.

De big Sunday School picnic   The Sunday School picnic that took place on a spring or summer day was often the biggest social event in a small community like Eatonville.

Chapter 12

Summary

The townsfolk become indignant when Janie, whom they consider to be Mrs. Mayor Starks, appears at a Sunday School picnic with Tea Cake. They become even more upset when Tea Cake and Janie begin to hunt, fish, dance, go to the movies, and seem to act like they are married.

One night, Pheoby and Sam Watson discuss the romance, and Sam sends Pheoby off to talk to Janie. Janie listens to her friend, but Pheoby's advice and caution are too late. Tea Cake is an independent and reliable man, and he is not after her money, Janie explains. She plans to live her life as she wants to live it, no longer following Nanny's wishes or Joe's control. Pheoby hints a bit of envy as she warns her friend about the risks of marrying Tea Cake.

Commentary

Theme

The theme of judgment returns in this chapter. Once again, the townspeople judge Janie. They believe that Joe has not been dead long enough for Janie to be involved with another man. They criticize her appearance and her actions, as well as her association with Tea Cake.

Finally, Janie is able to exercise her independence. She can make her own decisions; no one else will make them for her. More than anything, Janie wants to start anew. As she explains to Pheoby, "Ah done lived Grandma's way, now Ah means tuh live mine."

Character Insight

In this chapter, Pheoby proves herself to be a true friend to Janie. Like most of the townspeople, she fears that Tea Cake is after Janie's money. Pheoby approaches Janie and offers her friend advice, rather than gossip about her as the townspeople do. She is genuinely concerned about Janie's happiness.

Glossary

sense her into things   Sam Watson wants Pheoby to talk some common sense into Janie.

class off   act better than other people, show off.

He ain't got uh dime tuh cry   The townspeople are sure that Tea Cake has no money. Janie, however, knows he works and always pays their way.

Chapter 13

Summary

Janie boards a train in Eatonville and goes to Jacksonville to marry Tea Cake. It leaves too early in the morning for many of the townsfolk to see her depart, but those who do report to the others how beautiful she looked.

Tea Cake is a man of his word: They are quickly married. However, his first act as a new husband is to disappear with $200 of Janie's money. Janie has visions of her fate being similar to that of Mrs. Tyler, an Eatonville woman who was seduced—and then abandoned—by a younger man; afterwards, she returned to Eatonville in a totally decrepit condition.

After hours of Janie's fretting and worrying, a smiling and joking Tea Cake finally returns. He explains that he did not run off with another woman and that he never has any intention of doing so. He confesses that when he accidentally spied the money that Janie had brought along as a sort of personal insurance, he couldn't resist the temptation to throw a huge party for the men who worked on the railroad gangs with him and their wives and friends.

Tea Cake describes the party, making Janie laugh when he tells her about the two dollar admission he charged ugly women. Janie would have gone to the party, she says, if he had come back for her; he didn't do that, he says, because he thought that she wouldn't like the people. Janie assures him that she does not "class off." People are people to her, and she'll accept his friends.

The money that Tea Cake took from Janie will be replaced through Tea Cake's skill in gambling. Winning the money, however, involves some risk. When one loser objects to Tea Cake's pulling out of the game with all of the money, he stabs Tea Cake twice in the back. Janie doctors Tea Cake's wounds, which are fortunately only superficial. His winnings total more than $300. When his wounds are healed, he tells her, they'll leave Jacksonville and go to work on the muck in the Everglades, around Clewiston and Belle Glade, working in cane, bean, and tomato fields.

Commentary

This chapter marks the beginning of a new phase in Janie's life. She leaves the town of Eatonville behind, along with the memories of Joe Starks and the judgmental townspeople. Janie embarks on a new life with her new love, Tea Cake.

Although Janie is madly in love with Tea Cake, her greatest fear is that he will leave her for another woman. When Tea Cake disappears with Janie's money, her fear becomes evident as she remembers Mrs. Annie Tyler and her experience with a much younger man. Her panic "made itself into pictures and hung around Janie's bedside all night long." Janie wants to believe that Tea Cake will return to her, but she seems to focus on the worst, probably because she has not experienced a truly loving and healthy relationship in her life.

Theme

Hurston also highlights class differences in this chapter. Tea Cake reveals to Janie that he didn't invite her to his party because the people there were not "high muckety mucks." According to Tea Cake, "Dem wuz railroad hands and dey womenfolks." He fears that Janie would not be accepting of these people, simply because she has been playing the role of "Mrs. Mayor Joe Starks" for a while. Tea Cake wanted Janie to see "no commonness" in him. They are able to resolve these class differences when Janie reveals to Tea Cake that she wants to be with him, no matter where he is or who his friends are.

Yet again, Janie realizes her powerful love for Tea Cake, especially after his absence and his injuries. She feels a "self-crushing" love for her husband. It is at this point that Janie's "soul crawled out from its hiding place." Janie is no longer controlled by a domineering husband or an overprotective grandmother. Finally, she has found true love for the first time with Tea Cake.

Glossary

two hundred dollars inside her shirt   Janie is following some basic wisdom shared by wise women: Always have enough money on hand for your fare home—no matter who your date is.

twelve o'clock whistle   Jacksonville is a railroad town, and railroad shops usually had loud whistles that sounded at regular times during the day.

pink silk vest   Janie's "vest," or undershirt, is made of silk. Chances are that most of the women in Eatonville wore cotton underclothes.

round house   a circular house building, with a turntable in the center, used for storing and repairing locomotives.

Chapter 14

Summary

The Everglades and Lake Okeechobee are Tea Cake's territory. He knows the work, the bosses, the workers, and the camps. He and Janie arrive early so that they can get a room at a hotel where they will have access to a bathtub. Work in the muck is very dirty. They move on a few days later to a location where there is the assurance of work with a boss that Tea Cake likes. They rent a two-room house, which Janie soon turns into a home while Tea Cake plants beans. For diversion, Tea Cake proposes that he teach Janie how to handle guns and shoot.

The workers pour into the camp, but Tea Cake can't make any extra money gambling because this is the start of the season, and nobody has any money. The lively life of migrants surrounds Janie. These people work hard all day and play hard at night. The jook joints are alive with activity, and Tea Cake and Janie's house is an oasis for the other workers. Tea Cake sits in the doorway and entertains the people with his guitar and his stories.

At first, Janie only keeps house and cooks baked beans to please Tea Cake. When Janie grows tired of staying home and Tea Cake claims to be so lonesome for her that he has to take off work just to be with her, she decides to go to work with him. Together, they work and joke, and the migrants readily accept Janie. In the muck, Janie thinks about life in Eatonville and feels pity for the people there.

Commentary

In a short time, Janie gains acceptance from the other migrant workers, but only after enduring their initial judgments. After dealing with the boredom of keeping house and Tea Cake's loneliness for her, Janie decides to work in the fields with her husband. Many of the migrant workers believed that Janie "thought herself too good to work like the rest of the women." The workers pass judgment on Janie because she had not initially worked on the muck. They assumed that she considered herself too privileged to subject herself to the difficult labor of the migrant workers. She fits in quickly, and the judgments made by the workers are dropped as they witness the "romping and playing they [Tea Cake and Janie] carried on behind the boss's back."

Character Insight

Hurston also reveals in this chapter that Tea Cake serves to bring people together. His "house was a magnet, the unauthorized center of the 'job.'" Whether he plays the guitar or tells stories, the migrant workers seem to be drawn to Tea Cake and his charming personality, much like Janie is.

Unlike Janie's other husbands, Tea Cake makes a point to tell her that he loves her. He misses her so much while he is working in the fields that he convinces her to get a job working along side of him. Janie is the center of Tea Cake's world, and he does not want her to forget it.

Glossary

pickin' my box   playing my guitar.

dyke ... Indians   Hurston has inserted two seemingly insignificant details here which she will later use for dramatic effect when the hurricane strikes. Tea Cake and Janie live very close to the lake, and they will see Indians leaving as the storm approaches—yet they choose to ignore the wisdom of these local people.

jook   bar

flivver   a small, cheap automobile, especially an old one.

sit in the doorway   Hurston does not even suggest that the migrants go into Janie's house.

black-eyed peas and rice   This combination is known as "Hoppin' John." It is a staple with a long history in Southern cooking.

Chapter 15

Summary

One day, an overweight girl named Nunkie attempts to make a play for Tea Cake, and Janie is instantly jealous. Tea Cake goes through the motions of trying to resist the young girl, and Janie chases her away. When Tea Cake tries to talk to Janie, she hits him. A furious fight ensues, and when the dust is settled, she extracts assertions of his devotion to her.

Commentary

Janie becomes extremely jealous after she finds Nunkie flirting with Tea Cake in the fields. Although Janie feared that Tea Cake would leave her earlier when he disappeared with her $200, this time her fear is channeled into jealousy. This jealousy causes Janie to provoke a fight with Tea Cake so that he will be forced to remind her of his love for her.

Style & Language

Again, Hurston incorporates the image of the tree into the novel. This time, however, the tree image deals with Janie's fear that she will lose Tea Cake to another woman. As Janie witnesses the two in the fields, she feels anxious and upset. Janie's concern about Nunkie and Tea Cake's relationship grows, and she reveals that "a little seed of fear was growing into a tree." Janie needs reassurance from Tea Cake that he loves only her, and he will never leave her.

Glossary

snappish   cross or irritable, uncivil; sharp-tongued.

Don't keer how big uh lie get told, somebody kin b'lieve it
Tea Cake believes that the size of a lie has nothing to do with whether some people will believe it.

Chapter 16

Summary

Planting and harvesting are seasonal, and when the season ends, the migrants leave. Tea Cake and Janie stay on, and she becomes friendly with Mrs. Turner, an unattractive, overbearing woman who, with her mousy husband, runs a restaurant. The two women visit frequently, and Mrs. Turner expresses an attitude of bigotry that appalls Janie. Mrs. Turner has deep-seated prejudices against dark-complexioned people and rough migrants, even though they are her chief customers. Unlike Janie, Tea Cake feels angry and wounded about Mrs. Turner's bigotry. He vows to boycott the restaurant, but satisfactory eating places must have been in short supply because he and Janie continue to eat there.

Commentary

In this chapter, the character of Mrs. Turner is introduced. An unattractive, arrogant woman, Mrs. Turner, along with her husband, owns the local restaurant. She has deep-seated beliefs about the superiority of the Caucasian race. She and Janie had seen one another throughout the season, but they have not come to know one another until the season ended.

For the first time, Janie faces prejudice. Mrs. Turner only pursues a friendship with Janie because she has lighter skin than the rest of the migrant workers. She shares her strong beliefs with Janie as she tells her that "Ah can't stand black niggers . . . . Ah hates tuh see folks lak me and you mixed up wid 'em." Ironically, though, Mrs. Turner's livelihood depends on the support of the black migrant workers. The barrage of racist comments made by Mrs. Turner bewilders Janie. She also realizes that there is nothing that she can do to discourage Mrs. Turner from thinking the way that she does.

Style & Language

Hurston uses the image of an altar to relate Mrs. Turner's hatred for anyone who is not Caucasian. This altar represents the "unattainable—Caucasian characteristics for all." Mrs. Turner's beliefs are so strong that she would defend them at "the altars of her god." Through "worship," she hopes to "attain her paradise—a heaven of straight-haired, thin-lipped, high nose boned white seraphs." Hurston uses Mrs. Turner as an example of intolerance in the novel.

Glossary

Bahaman drummers   Hurston worked with Bahaman musicians in one of her theatrical efforts, and she used some of their nicknames for the characters in this novel.

Saws   another name for Bahamans.

meriny skin   like browned-egg-white meringue; a complexion color.

a vanishing-looking kind of man   Mr. Turner's presence is so insignificant that he seems about to vanish.

Chapter 17

Summary

Before long, the seasonal workers on the muck begin returning, and Mrs. Turner's brother arrives to chase after Janie, according to his sister's plan. It is then that Tea Cake conceives a plan that involves slapping Janie. For him, slapping his wife is an assertion of his role as a husband, and it is a gesture that the other migrants, as well as Mrs. Turner, will understand. Janie has been hit before, however. Joe struck her more than once.

A fight breaks out at Mrs. Turner's restaurant between several drunken migrant workers. Tea Cake joins the fight after he is unable to stop it. Mrs. Turner becomes angry with her husband because he failed to break up the brawl.

Commentary

Tea Cake begins to identify Janie as his possession. Because he feels threatened after Janie meets Mrs. Turner's brother, he strikes his wife to reassure himself that Janie belongs to him and no one else. Tea Cake doesn't believe that Janie did anything to deserve her beating; rather "it relieved that awful fear inside him." Also, Tea Cake wants to send a message to the Turners that he is in control. He confides to Sop-de-Bottom that it is Mrs. Turner's fault that he hit Janie because she sent her brother "tuh bait Janie in and take her away from me." Beating Janie stems from Tea Cake's need to control her, his jealousy, and the fear of losing his wife. Ironically, it is this type of control that caused Janie's isolation from Joe. In the beginning of her relationship with Tea Cake, he represented freedom for Janie. Now, however, Tea Cake is exerting the same domination over Janie that Joe did.

It is possible that Tea Cake and his friends allowed the fight to escalate into a brawl at the restaurant. Mrs. Turner angered Tea Cake when she sent her brother to try to lure Janie away from Tea Cake. Perhaps

Tea Cake and his friends hope that the physical damage caused at the restaurant will serve as an act of revenge for the emotional damage caused by Mrs. Turner's bigotry.

Glossary

peart   lively, chipper, sprightly, smart, and so on.

fracas   a noisy fight or loud quarrel; brawl.

Chapter 18

Summary

Late summer is hurricane season in the Everglades. Without taking the omens of the inevitable storm seriously, Tea Cake and Janie watch small groups of Seminoles leaving, heading toward Palm Beach Road and forsaking the money-making muck in order to survive the ominous, still invisible hurricane.

The fury does not wait long. In a sudden burst of thunder and lightning, the storm hits—and the world of Janie, Tea Cake, and the migrants is destroyed. As the people cluster together in fear of the elements, their eyes are not watching each other or the storm. In silent prayer, they are watching God. They make an effort to go to higher ground, but they are nearly swept away by the tremendous surge of water when the lake breaks through the dikes and surges toward them in a tall wall of rushing water. Tea Cake makes a valiant effort to keep Janie afloat by urging her to hang onto the tail of a cow. As the two struggle to survive the raging current, a rabid dog that is clinging to the cow bites Tea Cake on the cheek.

Commentary

Literary Device

The departure of the Seminoles from the muck foreshadows the arrival of the destructive hurricane. The migrant workers on the muck believe the Indians are wrong about the imminent storm, as fair weather continues, the beans are growing well, and prices are still fair. After the exit of the Seminoles, even the animals also head east, seemingly aware of the approaching hurricane. Still, though, Tea Cake, Janie, and most of the other migrant workers remain in the muck, unprepared for the threatening storm. "Money's too good on the muck" for Tea Cake to leave. Soon, these people will experience the destruction and terror associated with enduring a hurricane.

Hurston personifies the sea by comparing it to a monster that "began to roll in his bed." As the sea breaks through the dikes, Hurston reveals that "the monstropolous beast had left his bed" and continues on the path of destruction as the monster "was walking the earth with a heavy heel."

For the first time, Hurston uses the phrase that she also uses as the title for the novel. As Tea Cake, Janie and their friends try to wait out the storm at home, they wonder if God "meant to measure their puny might against His." The lights go out, the storm rages, and Tea Cake, Janie, and their friends "seemed to be staring at the dark, but their eyes were watching God." They realize that in the midst of such a powerful and destructive hurricane, they have no power to stop the storm. They must wait for it to end and hope that they will survive it.

Glossary

laden   loaded; burdened or afflicted.

stolid   having or showing little or no emotion or sensitivity; unexcitable; impassive.

money and insurance papers   This is further evidence that Tea Cake is a responsible man, even though he ignores the storm warnings and will be stubborn about not seeing a doctor.

Chapter 19

Summary

Janie and Tea Cake make it to safety in Palm Beach and survive, but Tea Cake is soon pressed into service by rifle-carrying white men who need him to help clear the wreckage and bury the dead. He and the other workers are instructed about the necessity of separating the bodies of white victims from the black corpses. The whites are to be buried in hastily constructed pine boxes; the blacks are just buried. As soon as Tea Cake has an opportunity to flee, he does so.

Janie is sincerely appreciative of her husband's efforts to save her life, and she urges him to see a doctor about the dog bite. Tea Cake refuses, insisting that, first of all, they need to find a place to rest. Janie is proud of his heroism, and he wants her to know that she has a real man to take care of her. Shortly thereafter, they decide to go back to the muck. Tea Cake has had enough of Palm Beach; the city is too inhospitable.

Back on the muck, Tea Cake checks up on his old friends and is relieved to learn that only one of them died in the storm. He soon finds work, and after three weeks, he and Janie take time off to enjoy rifle shooting. Some time later, Tea Cake begins to show signs of an infection where the dog bit him on the cheek. Janie tries to take care of him, but as his illness progresses, he becomes more difficult. His inability to swallow water frightens both of them. Janie leaves to fetch Doctor Simmons, a white doctor, for her desperately ill husband, but it is too late. The doctor will be able to get the serum, but nothing can help Tea Cake now.

In the fury of his illness, he struggles with Janie. Hopelessly deranged, he suddenly threatens her with the six-shooter, and she defends herself with the rifle. His pistol and her rifle fire simultaneously. Tea Cake falls forward and buries his teeth in Janie's forearm, as she catches him. Later, Janie must endure a brief trial, but she is freed. Afterward, she must arrange his funeral. She gives Tea Cake a glorious send-off, burying him in Palm Beach. This time there is real mourning for the dead.

Commentary

Theme

For the second time in the novel, Hurston hints at the occurrence of racism. All of the white people who died in the hurricane will be buried in coffins, while the black people will just be buried. The guards instructing Tea Cake on how to bury the dead explain that the coffins are "too hard tuh git holt of right now" to be wasted on the bodies of the deceased blacks. Tea Cake is troubled by the double standard created by the intolerant guards. With his first opportunity, Tea Cake escapes, and he confides to Janie that they must leave immediately because he "don't mean tuh work lak dat no mo'."

As Tea Cake becomes seriously ill, Janie reflects on the rabid dog that caused her husband's illness. Somehow she doesn't find Tea Cake's fate fair, as he was just trying to protect her when the dog bit him. Watching her husband die, Janie says, is too much for her to bear, and she wishes that the dog had killed her instead. Janie questions and pleads with God, wondering why "Tea Cake, the son of Evening Sun, had to die for loving her."

Style & Language

While Tea Cake's funeral is similar to Joe's in that they both were given a distinguished farewell, one aspect remains different. This time Janie does not wear traditional mourning attire to the service; rather, she wears her overalls, clothing that she associates with her husband. Tea Cake's awful death devastates Janie, and she confesses that "she was too busy feeling grief to dress like grief." In contrast to Joe's funeral, Janie does not look like a widow at Tea Cake's funeral, but she certainly feels the sorrow and the pain of being one.

Glossary

Tryin' not to keep you outa yo' comfortable no longer'n you wanted to stay In other words, I don't want to keep you here in this uncomfortable place any longer than you want to stay. Earlier in the novel, Tea Cake wanted to comb Janie's hair, and she referred to it as her "comfortable," not his. "Comfortable" would be a unique personal possession.

Give it uh poor man's trial A poor man takes any respectable job he can get and does his best with it.

uh common trial   similar to the definition above. Just to be working, Tea Cake will take any job available.

de Jim Crow law   These are laws associated with traditional discrimination against or segregation of blacks, especially in the United States.

trouble and compellment   Tea Cake is troubled by the white guards forcing him—compelling him—to help bury the dead.

motherless chile   Tea Cake is out of his element. He feels as though he doesn't belong to anyone, like a child in slavery sold away from its mother. The song "Sometimes I Feel Like a Motherless Child" is often included in collections of spirituals.

Six months behind de United States privy house at hard smellin'   The reference is to a privy, a toilet, especially an outhouse, which has a thoroughly obnoxious smell if it hasn't been properly maintained. This is Tea Cake's metaphor for being tossed into a federal jail and put to hard work.

bucked each other   beat and/or challenged each other.

quart of coon-dick   cheap moonshine or bootleg whiskey.

lap-legged brother   a suggestion that Mrs. Turner's brother's legs are malformed and not straight—clearly, an insult.

watchin' de job   watching and waiting for Tea Cake to die.

relic   Janie is the relic, or the person who has survived, from their marriage. The word could also be an echo of the Old English term relict, which means surviving the death of another.

Chapter 20

Summary

Because the people were so fond of Tea Cake, Janie stays a few more weeks in the Everglades, but home to her is still Eatonville. Thus, she returns from the Everglades in the overalls she wore to work on the muck. Now, the frame of Janie's story is complete. Pheoby reacts to Janie's tale by promising herself that she and Sam will spend more time together. Janie's story has indeed inspired her.

Commentary

After Tea Cake's funeral, Janie stays in the Everglades, but it is too painful for her there, as the place only reminds her of her beloved husband. Janie gives away everything she owns except for a package of garden seed, a reminder of Tea Cake and his love for planting things. Janie plans to plant the seeds to serve as a symbol of the love and the life that they shared.

Literary Device

Janie's flashback ends, and the novel returns to Janie's conversation with Pheoby that began in Chapter 1. It is almost as if Janie's life story could serve as a lesson both to her dear friend, Pheoby, and to the readers of the novel. In her journey through life, Janie has learned two important lessons: People must "go tuh God," and they must "find out about livin' fuh theyselves."

Finally, Janie realizes that as long as she lives, the memory of Tea Cake will live within her heart. By the end of the novel, Janie has found the peace that she has desired for her entire life.

Glossary

Love is lak de sea . . . it's different with every shore   Hurston uses the simile to explain that love is different for everyone who experiences it.

fetid   having a bad smell, as of decay; putrid.

commence   to begin; start; originate.

CHARACTER ANALYSES

Janie Crawford Killicks Starks Woods

An unwritten law in the little community in which Janie Crawford grew up stated that no girl would appear in school better dressed than the other girls, even those wearing second-hand clothes. Likewise, no 16-year-old should live in a neat little house with a yard on land owned by her grandmother. Moreover, no young girl should have a coffee-and-cream complexion and a long braid of dark hair that hangs below her waist. Surely such a child would think herself better than her schoolmates, and later, better than other women. The exception to that unwritten law is Janie Crawford, who continually finds herself being defined by other people rather than by herself—even from the beginning.

For Nanny, Janie's grandmother, Janie represents a second chance to do something right with a child. Born to Nanny's daughter, 17-year-old Leafy who was raped by the town schoolteacher, little Janie grows up as her grandmother's special child. Her father had disappeared long ago, and her mother abandoned her shortly afterward.

Janie's early childhood years are spent in Nanny's household, playing with the white grandchildren of Mrs. Washburn, Nanny's benevolent white employer. Not until she is 6 years old does she realize that she is a brown-skinned little girl—and not white like her Washburn playmates. She is an outsider at school, taunted by the other girls who envy her clothing, her complexion, and her extraordinary hair. Without giving Janie a chance to be friendly, the girls decide that she considers herself better that they are. Janie makes no friends at school.

Nanny encourages this attitude of exceptionality in Janie. The old woman labors not for herself, but for this child whom she believes that God has sent to her. With the help of Mrs. Washburn, Nanny buys some land and a house—more for Janie than for herself, thereby enhancing Janie's role as a very special person.

In her first marriage to the farmer Logan Killicks, Janie, at age sixteen, begins to draw some lines in her own way. Logan sees her as a spoiled child who must learn to be a farm wife. It is quite evident that Janie is willing to perform the chores that she sees as rightfully and dutifully hers, but those chores do not include plowing a potato field, regardless of how gentle the mule is. Although Logan recognizes the special qualities that Janie carries within herself, he fails to respect Janie as his wife. She desires a better life, and Janie believes that she will find it with Joe Starks.

Joe, the third person in Janie's life, wants her because he sees that she has class. She is a physically attractive young woman, far above any other woman Joe has known. He takes her as a possession, a trophy he has captured and can display along with his other possessions: his town, his house, his store, and his position as mayor.

Neither Nanny nor Joe ever consults Janie about what she wants in life; therefore, Janie is always yearning for something. The inner Janie is far from satisfied. Within the outwardly attractive woman called Janie Starks is a simple inner woman called Janie, and all she wants is to love and to be loved.

After Joe dies, when Janie is in her late 30s and economically secure and free, Tea Cake Woods comes strolling down the road with his guitar and his fun-loving ways. Like a true romantic hero, he courts Janie, a new and exciting experience for her. All he can offer her is his guitar, his songs, his mischievous spirit, and jobs on the muck of the Everglades with a gang of migrant workers. It is enough for Janie.

In a way, Tea Cake, like the others, defines Janie, but not in a restrictive way. In this marriage, Janie finds the love she sought in other relationships. Tea Cake is a man who respects Janie as an intelligent, exciting companion.

In addition to the security of Tea Cake's love, Janie is eventually accepted unconditionally and is not judged by the migrant workers. Nanny, Joe, and the Eatonville porch sitters would have said that the workers on the muck were unbearably crude people, but Janie accepts them as fellow human beings. Because of the brief time that she spends with Tea Cake on the muck, Janie transcends the misery of being defined by someone else and discovers who she is, what she can do, and how fulfilling love can be.

Nanny

Janie's grandmother has no name. She is simply "Nanny" to Janie because that is what the white children that she takes care of call her. Born into slavery, Nanny tells Janie her life story when the girl is sixteen. Her experiences make her sadly aware of what can happen to an attractive woman. Her daughter, Leafy, was the product of the attentions of a white master. Nanny fled the plantation to escape a brutal beating promised by her mistress. Soon afterward, she experienced the excitement of emancipation, and she found a place in Florida where she could live, work, and raise her daughter. This child, she hoped, would become a schoolteacher. Her hopes were dashed when Leafy was raped, ironically by the town schoolteacher, who abandoned both mother and child.

Nanny's life revolves around her love for Janie and her loyalty to her employer, Mrs. Washburn. Within the limits of this small world, Nanny is an ambitious woman. With the help of Mrs. Washburn, she buys land and a little house, an unusual undertaking for a lone woman. She has aspirations for Janie, who has never had to work in a white woman's kitchen because Nanny did that labor for her.

Without a doubt, Nanny loves Janie, but it is a love based on duty and responsibility. It may be a transference of the dreams that she never achieved for herself. In any case, the two women need each other, because they have no other family. All Nanny asks for in return is that Janie grow up to be a decent girl.

When Janie comes to her with questions about the kind of love that should exist between husband and wife, Nanny can provide no answers. That sort of love has never been a part of her own life. Logan Killicks can offer this child security with his 60-acre potato farm. Nanny sees no need for the love that Janie asks about.

A month after this conversation, Nanny is dead, and Janie is alone and unloved.

Logan Killicks

Through Janie's unhappy comments, we learn that Logan Killicks is an old, unattractive man. Nanny, however, sees him as security for Janie. A hard-working farmer with 60 acres of land and a comfortable house, Logan does not have a major part in Janie's story, and yet he is a significant person in the culture of the South. He owns his own land, and he farms it successfully. He comes to call on Nanny, seeking what can be described only as a replacement for his first wife. Not until Nanny agrees to his marrying Janie does Janie realize why Logan has been coming around the house so often.

Back on the farm with his new, young wife, Logan continues to follow the demanding farm routines, and he does certain household chores as well, because he considers them to be his responsibility. He keeps the water buckets full and chops wood for the stove. These are acts of love that Logan understands. Janie, however, wants a different kind of love, one that begins with clean feet and trimmed toenails. In contrast, Logan needs more help from his bride with the outside work. For him, love is giving Janie a gentle mule so that she can help him plow the fields.

Logan is old and set in his ways; farm routines control his life. He knows Janie is a spoiled girl, and he is unable to understand the depth of her boredom. Soon after he plods off to get a gentle mule, Janie meets Joe Starks. It is not long before she leaves Logan complaining in the barnyard, returns to the house, and escapes down the road to meet Joe and to follow his dream. No more references are made to Logan in Janie's life.

Joe Starks

If Joe Starks has one outstanding trait, it is confidence. From the moment he meets Janie until his death nearly 20 years later, he never doubts his ability to accomplish his goals. He can persuade people to believe in his dreams, accept his management, and give him loyalty. Although the porch sitters grumble behind his back about his high-pressure ways, they have to concede his skill in creating their town, Eatonville.

Physically, Joe is not especially overpowering. He is probably a man of average size and dark complexion, one who puts weight on as he nears middle age. He characteristically smokes a cigar. No other man in this novel smokes; the cigar is Joe's signature, the indication that he is the manager and mayor—different from the farmers and laborers of the town.

Joe is a dreamer of very pragmatic dreams, if such a contradiction can be presented. He brings money, charisma, and a young bride to a developing town. No one else has thought about adding acreage to the town, but Joe goes boldly off to the white landowner and comes back with the deed to 200 acres.

Having thus attracted attention, Joe calls a meeting and gets himself elected mayor. The next step is the construction of a crossroads store and the establishment of a U.S. government post office. Joe's extraordinary self-confidence leads to control, a manifestation of power. One sure object of his control is Janie. He defines the role he expects her to play, and it is one of subservience. Any idea of consulting her about his enterprises is far from his mind. He finds it easy to belittle her in front of the porch sitters because of her incompetence at doing calculations in the store and post office. Furthermore, Janie is not allowed to join the fun of the game of checkers because Joe has decided that she is not smart enough to play the game.

Joe did not marry Janie for love; he married her for show. Power—control of people, position, property, and even money—rules Joe Starks. For Joe, love is self-love. Janie is a handsome accessory to the glory that surrounds Joe Starks.

Vergible "Tea Cake" Woods

Tea Cake comes strolling into Eatonville hoping to watch a baseball game. Instead, he finds the widow Janie Starks minding her store while just about everyone else in town has left to go to the ballgame. He arrives a happy man, and his happiness attracts Janie. That is all author Hurston, with her tendency to shortchange her readers about the physical descriptions of her characters, tells us. He is some 12 years younger than Janie.

Tea Cake, having appeared from nowhere and seeming to have no visible means of support, worries the porch sitters because they are sure he is after Janie's money. He is just as independent as Joe Starks, but he doesn't seem interested in building towns or stores or acquiring possessions. He makes it clear to Janie, though, that he will work and take care of her. Cautiously, but excited by his presence, Janie accepts his courtship.

Courtship is part of the music of Tea Cake's life. Tea Cake treats Janie like a special person, not because she still carries with her that aura of class, but because some masculine instinct tells him that if he wants her, he will have to woo her. Tea Cake has the personality to make Janie think that maybe this man might give her the sort of love for which she has been waiting.

Tea Cake leads Janie to discover things about herself she never knew in her years with Nanny, Logan, or Joe. He teaches her how to play checkers, how to handle guns, and how to shoot. They go on picnics, much to the dismay of the porch sitters, who resent his intrusion on Janie's mandatory mourning period. He listens to Janie's opinions, helps her in the store, and plays his guitar for her. The porch sitters' gossip, but they don't challenge him.

Tea Cake's pride comes from self-confidence, just as did Joe's. Tea Cake knows he is a good gambler. He knows he is a competent worker on the muck. He knows he can provide for his wife, and he knows that he will be faithful to her. He is, in an unassuming way, a leader among the migrants on the muck. Unlike Joe, Tea Cake's self-confidence is not combined with ambition; unlike Joe, he can openly express his love for Janie. He is able to give her the dream of love that Joe Starks never understood.

Even Tea Cake's death contrasts with Joe's. Tea Cake's heroism on the muck while they try to outrun the hurricane ultimately led to his demise. Joe, however, endured a slow, painful death. His death was not valiant like Tea Cake's. Hurston presents Tea Cake as the hero, the man with whom the reader sympathizes.

Pheoby Watson

Pheoby Watson is Janie's best friend and confidante. She sits on the porch of the store or her own home and listens to the gossipy busy-bodies meddling in Janie's life. They talk, both the men and the women, and Pheoby has many ways of suggesting that they don't know what they're talking about. However, it is often her husband, Sam, who tells them to be quiet.

Unlike the other women who watch the dirty and disheveled Janie return home, Pheoby is not ready with instant condemnation. Instead, she senses that Janie has a story to tell and that she's probably hungry. Pheoby wisely takes a bowl of mulatto rice to her friend, knowing for sure that Janie will talk to her. Her motive for taking food is not totally unselfish. She wants to know why Janie has come home.

Janie knows the depth of Pheoby's loyalty, and she also knows that she may explain matters to the porch sitters. However, the choice of telling or not telling and the way it will be told, if she chooses to tell it, will be left up to Pheoby. Pheoby does not show the jealousy of Janie that characterizes the other women. She is emotionally close to Janie, and they share many experiences, one of which is fishing. It is reasonable to assume that her husband, Sam, is too well established in the town for the busybodies to gossip about him or his wife. Happy with Sam and comfortable about herself, Pheoby has no reason to be jealous of anyone.

After listening to her friend's story, Pheoby understands that there can be rich experiences in the remaining years of her own marriage. She will try to open up her life with Sam, and they will do more things together.

Pheoby leaves Janie's back steps, refreshed by the story she has heard, and Janie goes into her lonely house, confident that she can trust her friend in the retelling of the story.

Sam Watson

Sam Watson is undeniably a rank-and-file porch sitter, although he is often impatient with the gossips who gather on the porch. He is Pheoby's husband, and often he and Pheoby are buffers between Janie and the porch sitters. Sam's voice is one of moderation; his attitude is one of tolerance. He is most likely to speak up to defend Janie against the evil suspicions of the porch sitters, and he is often willing to chase the crowd from his porch when he tires of the chatter. He is a man with a pleasant sense of humor. Hurston does not tell her readers what work Sam does; his occupation is not important. His impatience with the porch sitters and his support of Janie are.

How will Sam respond when Pheoby impulsively tells him she wants to go on a picnic or go fishing on a summer afternoon? Chances are, Sam will think about it for a moment and then haul out the fishing lines.

The Porch Sitters

The front porch of Joe Starks' crossroads store is the gathering place for many of the men and women of Eatonville. There they sit or lean against the railing, sipping soft drinks, eating cheese and soda crackers, talking, and talking. When their day's work is over, that's one way to pass the time. The porch sitters at the store are most likely to be men. The women usually gather on the porch of someone's home, maybe Pheoby Watson's, to gossip. Their excuse to be on the store porch may be to play checkers or to watch a game of checkers being played. The real reason, of course, is to talk and tease.

Having created this group, Hurston gives them names, and they have dignified family names, not colorful, exotic names like the men on the muck. As individuals, with the exceptions of Sam and Pheoby, they are not significant characters. As a group, they may be seen as functioning as a sort of chorus. They serve as modern commentators giving their own interpretations to the actions of the main characters and providing an interlude, as in the mule story.

The Migrants

In contrast to the Eatonville porch sitters who have standard names, most of Tea Cake and Janie's friends in the muck have such colorful nicknames as Stew Beef, Coodemay, and Sop-de-Bottom. After the hurricane had ravaged the area and Tea Cake and Janie return to the muck, they are relieved and surprised to discover that all of their friends, except one, survived the fury of the storm.

In contrast to the Eatonville men, who are hard workers in a stable community, the muck people are migrant farm laborers who live from day to day, crop to crop, season to season. They are as much a community as the people of Eatonville, but they spend their leisure time drinking, gambling, dancing in the jook joints (unheard of in pious Eatonville), and fighting. Living on the edge, moving around so much, life is a day-to-day affair for them. Tomorrow is the next crop, the next migrant camp.

Along with this apparent lightheartedness is a great deal of care and concern for members of their group, as is shown in the respect they have for Janie and Tea Cake and the drastic action—the staged brawl—they take against Mrs. Turner and her bigotry.

CRITICAL ESSAYS

Love, Independence, and Judgment as Major Themes in *Their Eyes Were Watching God*

The most prevalent themes in *Their Eyes Were Watching God* involve Janie's search for unconditional, true, and fulfilling love. She experiences different kinds of love throughout her life. As a result of her quest for this love, Janie gains her own independence and personal freedom, which makes her a true heroine in the novel. Because Janie strives for her own independence, others tend to judge her simply because she is daring enough to achieve her own autonomy.

Throughout the novel, Janie searches for the love that she has always desired, the kind of love that is represented by the marriage between a bee and a blossom on the pear tree that stood in Nanny's backyard. Only after feeling other kinds of love does Janie finally gain the love like that between the bee and the blossom.

Janie experiences many types of love throughout her life. With Nanny, her caring grandmother, Janie experiences a love that is protective. Nanny yearns for Janie to have a better life than she did, and she will do anything in her power to make sure that Janie is safe and cared for. This protective love that Nanny bestows on Janie serves as the driving force behind Nanny's plot to arrange Janie's marriage to Logan Killicks.

With Logan, Janie has attained a similarly protective love, much like that provided by Nanny. Logan represents security for Janie, as he owns a 60-acre potato farm. For Janie, however, this protective love does not satisfy her need for the love that she has always desired.

Joe Starks provides Janie with an escape from the protective and unsatisfying love of Logan. Joe is a man with lofty goals and charisma. Janie feels for the first time in her life that she may be able to find true love with this man who wants her to be treated like a lady, rather than as a subservient farmer's wife. After being married just a short time, however, Janie realizes that she is once again lacking the love that she has longed for. The love that Janie experiences with Joe is a possessive love. Joe views Janie as his possession, his trophy wife. He expects Janie to follow his orders, just as the townspeople abide by the laws he creates as mayor. Joe forbids Janie to interact with the porch sitters or to play checkers on the porch of the crossroads store. Janie feels trapped by Joe's love, but she remains with him until his death.

Following Joe's death, Janie meets the man who represents the true love of her life, Tea Cake Woods. He arrives in Eatonville as a fun-loving man who quickly falls for Janie's beauty and charm. Although Janie fears that she is too old for Tea Cake, she cannot help but fall in love with this man. Janie leaves behind everything that she has ever known to embark on a new life with Tea Cake. She adores him, as he adores her. After moving to the Everglades with Tea Cake, she embraces this new life as well as her new friends. Finally, Janie has found the love like that between the bee and its blossom. She declares that Tea Cake could be a "bee to a blossom—a pear tree blossom in the spring."

In her search for love and in the losses that she suffers, Janie gains independence. Janie's independence begins slowly in the novel. She holds a spark of independence when she gains the courage to leave her loveless marriage with Logan in order to run away with Joe Starks. Her independence grows, however, throughout her marriage to Joe. As Joe treats Janie as his possession instead of his wife, Janie gains an inner strength. Her strength builds, and one day she stands up for herself to Joe in the presence of the porch sitters. This act is Janie's first outward sign of her inner strength. Her strength and independence grow as Joe becomes weaker. Although he banishes Janie from his room, she visits him anyway. As Joe lies dying, Janie reveals to him that he is not the man that she ran off with years ago. She tells Joe that he has never been able to accept her for the person that she really is. Ironically, Janie finds strength in Joe's death. Finally, she is free of the man who confined her in a loveless marriage. Janie exhibits her freedom after Joe's death by removing the kerchief from her head to let her long braids drape freely down her back.

Throughout Janie's quest for love and the independence that she gains in her journey, Janie endures the harsh judgment of others. The porch sitters in the novel serve to judge Janie. As the novel opens, they sit and comment about Janie's return and her present lifeless appearance. The theme of judgment continues in Janie's life with Joe. He judges Janie, rather than accepting her for what and who she is. He stifles her independence because he fears that another man may take her away from him. Even Mrs. Turner, the bigoted restaurant owner, judges Janie. She questions Janie's choice of Tea Cake as a husband, because he is "too black." Because Janie endures the harsh judgments of others, she is able to gain independence and strength.

Janie's quest for love leads her along different paths. She gains strength from the protective love of Nanny and Logan as well as the possessive love of Joe. Janie finds her desired love with Tea Cake. Throughout her life, she also gains an independence and strength from these relationships as well as by enduring the judgments made by others. As a result of her lifelong encounters, Janie gains autonomy and learns the value of true love. As a character, Janie proves herself as a heroine.

Hurston created the character of Janie during a time in which African-American female heroines were uncommon in literature. In 1937 when the novel was originally published, females experienced fewer opportunities than they do today. Hurston chose to portray Janie as a strong, independent woman, unlike most African-American females of the early nineteenth century. Perhaps Hurston characterized Janie as capable and courageous to empower her readers and to show them that opportunities do exist for all women; they just have to embrace them.

Framing the Story: The Unique Structure of *Their Eyes Were Watching God*

Their Eyes Were Watching God possesses a unique structure. The story is told in the context of a "frame." The novel both begins and ends with two people, Janie and Pheoby, sitting on the porch of Janie's house. Janie tells the stories contained within the novel to Pheoby during the course of an evening. The novel begins with Janie telling her dear friend, Pheoby, about what has happened in the years since she left Eatonville, along with reflections of her childhood. As the story proceeds chronologically, however, the story is not a first-person narrative. Hurston takes over the narrative with the use of third-person point of view. The reader encounters Janie's experiences as Janie faced them, yet Hurston controls the story.

Within the novel, there are four units to the framework of the story. The first frame exists with Janie's childhood and adolescent years with her grandmother, Nanny. The reader learns that Nanny was forced to care for Janie after her own mother deserted her. This portion of the novel is important as it details Nanny's wish for Janie that she have a better life than she did. This unit also is significant because it emphasizes Nanny's protective love for Janie. It also explores Janie's feelings and desires about love, a theme that continues throughout the novel.

The second unit serves as an interlude where readers learn Nanny's story as well as Janie's loss of childhood after her marriage to Logan Killicks. Nanny's history proves noteworthy as it reinforces her hopes for Janie. Nanny does not want Janie to repeat the mistakes of her mother. She wants Janie to live a secure and comfortable life. Nanny is not as concerned about love as Janie is. Perhaps that is because Nanny has never experienced the kind of love that Janie desires. This unit also emphasizes Nanny's protective love for Janie.

Janie's years with Joe Starks fill the third section of the framework in the novel. This unit represents Janie's early happiness with Joe as well as her later dissatisfaction with Joe as he treats her like one of his many possessions. Janie suffers from Joe's possessive love as she is trapped in a loveless relationship. Joe's control over Janie actually fosters her strength and autonomy. However, it is also in this section that Janie gains the inner strength that she will use throughout the rest of the novel.

The fourth and final section of the novel focuses on Janie's marriage to Tea Cake. Finally, Janie has experienced freedom and independence following Joe's death. She meets the captivating and charming Tea Cake and finds the love that she has desired since her adolescent years. He satisfies her desire for love, and she experiences true happiness for the first time. With Tea Cake, Janie is no longer the possession that she was to Joe, and the love that she feels is not based solely on security and protection. This fourth unit brings the novel to the end of the frame.

The framework of the novel is complete as Janie's recollections and stories end and Pheoby returns home to her husband. It is through Janie's eyes that the reader understands the story. Yet, Hurston tells the story in third person to allow the reader to know more about the other characters and their perspectives.

It is possible that Hurston chose to tell the story within a framework to give Janie a voice in the novel. Had Hurston relied solely on a third person narrative, Janie would have had no voice. Using first person narrative in this framework proves that Janie has gained strength and independence as a result of her lifelong search for true love.

Figurative Language in *Their Eyes Were Watching God*

Hurston uses many symbols and metaphors in *Their Eyes Were Watching God* to develop Janie's story. Symbols stand for, represent, or suggest another thing. A metaphor, however, is a figure of speech containing an implied comparison, in which a word or phrase ordinarily and primarily used for one thing is applied to another.

One of the prevalent metaphors in the novel is the image of the horizon. As Janie climbs the pear tree to see what exists around her, she sees the horizon. The horizon also plays a role at sundown, a time when the porch sitters sit outside at the end of a working day to watch the sun set. Janie wants to make a trip to the horizon, and her journey becomes a principal metaphor in the story. At sunrise, Janie travels down the road to the train station to meet and marry Tea Cake, hoping that this experience will take her to the horizon. The horizon is a symbol of Janie's lifelong search for happiness. At the end of the story, Pheoby is anxious to seek her own horizon with her husband, as a result of hearing Janie's story.

Another metaphor in the novel can be found in the working men and women and the comparison to the mule. The men sitting on the porches have been working all day and have been treated like mules throughout the working day. Only at the end of the day as they enjoy their leisure time on the porch do they become human beings. In Hurston's interlude of the mule, the animal is given respite near the end of his life, just as the hard-working men and women "mules" get respite at the end of their working day.

A second image of a mule exists in the novel. Matt Bonner's mule also represents mistreatment and betrayal. Perhaps Janie feels sympathy for the poor animal because she, too, suffers the effects of abuse, just as the mule does. While the mistreatment that Janie endures is primarily emotional, the abuse that the mule experiences is mostly physical. Regardless of the type of mistreatment each faces, the mule exists as a symbol of the abuse that Janie encounters in her marriage to Joe.

One of the most powerful metaphors in the novel is the blossoming pear tree. Janie is enchanted by the beautiful tree in Nanny's backyard. As she climbs the tree and sits in its branches, Janie realizes the meaning of true love when she sees the marriage of the bees to the blossoms in the pear tree. The blossoming pear tree symbolizes Janie's emerging womanhood. Janie's image of love, as she saw it in the pear tree, causes her to embark on her lifelong search for love.

Hurston's Use of Dialect in *Their Eyes Were Watching God*

Hurston uses dialect to bring the story as well as the characters to life. The use of dialect makes the characters seem real; they are believable. After making some initial adjustments as a reader to become familiar with the language, readers feel as if they were actually a part of the action.

It is worth noting that the dialect used in the novel is closer to a Southern dialect, rather than an African-American dialect. Not only do Janie, Tea Cake, and their friends have similar speech patterns, but also the guards who command Tea Cake after the hurricane speak in a comparable dialect. Hurston's familiarity with the language of the South enables her to accurately depict the dialect of the region.

Their Eyes Were Watching God is rich in dialect, known as the spoken version of a language. Dialect is regional, and it has distinctive features of vocabulary, grammar, and pronunciation. Early in the novel, Hurston tells her readers what to expect in the language of her characters. She states that Janie will tell her story to Pheoby in "soft, easy phrases." Readers unfamiliar with such phrases often see Hurston's language as a strange dialect and a barrier to enjoying the novel. Once readers understand the dialect and its common features, the text becomes familiar and easy to read.

The reader approaches both Eatonville and the muck as an outsider and soon discovers patterns in the language of the characters. Initial and final consonants are frequently dropped. "You" becomes "yuh," occasionally "y'all," a plural. "I" is invariably "Ah." Vowel shifts also occur often. For example, "get" becomes "git." The final "r" is "ah." "Us" may occur as the nominative, and verbs, especially auxiliary verbs, are generally left out. A double negative such as "Nobody don't know" gives emphasis. Distortions of the past tense also occur. For example, "knew" becomes "knowed." Because "–ed" is a sign of the simple past, it is logical in dialect to add "-ed" to make a past tense verb. The reflexive pronoun "himself" becomes "hisself." A final "th" is spoken as "f," and although the final "r" is softened in some words, it is added to others. In addition to patterns of dialect, Janie and her friends speak a language rich in a vocabulary of localisms and folklore references. These features are also characteristic of regional speech and help make dialects distinctive.

The character of Tea Cake is to some extent characterized by his language. He is the only character who consistently uses "us" as a nominative; perhaps it is Hurston's subtle way of suggesting that Tea Cake is of a lower class than Joe or the porch sitters.

CliffsNotes Review

Use this CliffsNotes Review to test your understanding of the original text and reinforce what you've learned in this book. After you work through the review and essay questions, identify the quote section, and the fun and useful practice projects, you're well on your way to understanding a comprehensive and meaningful interpretation of Zora Neale Hurston's *Their Eyes Were Watching God.*

Fill in the Blank

1. Nanny arranges for Janie to marry _____.

2. After leaving her first husband, Janie marries _____ and they head to _____ to establish a new town.

3. The _____ gossip on the porch of the crossroads store.

4. A young, fun-loving man, _____, arrives in town and catches Janie's attention.

5. Janie marries her third husband and they move to _____ to work _____.

6. A _____ causes devastation and it forces Janie and her husband to run for their lives.

7. _____ ultimately causes the illness that contributes to Tea Cake's death.

8. _____, Janie's best friend, listens to Janie tell the story of her life.

Answers: (1) Logan Killicks. (2) Joe Starks; Eatonville, Florida. (3) porch sitters. (4) Vergible "Tea Cake" Woods. (5) the Everglades; on the "muck". (6) hurricane. (7) a bite from a rabid dog. (8) Pheoby.

Multiple Choice

1. When Pheoby visits Janie, she takes her

   a. a pan of cornbread.

   b. a pot of beans.

   c. a pot of mulatto rice.

   d. a pan of sweet potato muffins.

2. When Janie lived with her grandmother, Nanny, they lived on the property of Nanny's employer. Who was she?

    a. Mrs. Washington

    b. Mrs. Washburn

    c. Mrs. Smith

    d. Mrs. Franklin

3. Janie's first husband, Logan is a _____ farmer.

    a. dairy

    b. peanut

    c. soybean

    d. potato

4. Matt Bonner is accused of mistreating his

    a. mule.

    b. cat.

    c. dog.

    d. cow.

5. Tea Cake teaches Janie to play

    a. tic tac toe.

    b. checkers.

    c. hopscotch.

    d. chess.

6. Janie feels jealous when _____ makes a play for Tea Cake.

    a. Mrs. Turner

    b. Mary

    c. Pheoby

    d. Nunkie

7. _____ manages the restaurant in the Everglades. She expresses an attitude of bigotry that appalls Janie.

    a. Mrs. Turner

    b. Mrs. Washburn

    c. Nanny

    d. Pheoby

Answers: (1) c. (2) b. (3) d. (4) a. (5) b. (6) d. (7) a.

Identify the Quote

1. "They know mo' 'bout yuh than you do yo' self. . . . They done 'heard' 'bout you just what they hope done happened."

2. "Ah wanted yuh to school out and pick from a higher bush and a sweeter berry."

3. "You done been spoilt rotten."

4. "A pretty doll-baby lak you is made to sit on de front porch and rock and fan yo'self and eat p'taters dat other folks plant just special for you."

5. "Speakin' of winds, he's de wind and we'se de grass. We bend which ever way he blows . . . but at dat us needs him."

6. "It's so easy to make yo'self out God Almighty when you ain't got nothing tuh strain against but women and chickens."

7. "You changes everything but nothin' don't change you—not even death."

8. "Nobody else on earth kin hold uh candle tuh you, baby. You got de keys to de kingdom."

9. "If you kin see de light at daybreak, you don't keer if you die at dusk. It's so many people never seen de light at all. Ah wuz fumblin' round and God opened de door."

10. "Two things everybody's got tuh do fuh theyselves. They got tuh go tuh God, and they got to find out about livin' fuh theyselves."

Answers: (1) Pheoby to Janie, regarding the porch sitters and their gossip about what has happened to Janie since she left Eatonville. (2) Nanny to Janie, explaining that she wants her granddaughter to have a better life than she has experienced and she wants Janie to marry Logan Killicks. (3) Logan to Janie, as he explains that his first wife had helped him with the farm chores. (4) Joe to Janie, explaining that she should not be laboring on the farm; she should be treated like a lady. (5) Sam Watson to Sim Jones, Oscar Scott, Jeff Bruce, and Hicks, about Joe Starks becoming mayor of Eatonville. (6) Janie to Joe, in front of porch sitters after Joe's interaction with Mrs. Robbins. (7) Janie to Joe, just before he dies. (8) Tea Cake to Janie, as he confesses his true feelings for love for her. (9) Janie to Tea Cake, during the hurricane. (10) Janie to Pheoby, as she finishes the story of her life at the end of the novel.

Essay Questions

1. Throughout Janie's life, she searches for true, unconditional love. In her search, she experiences different kinds of love. Describe the types of love she experiences. Which type of love has the most impact on her life? In the end, has Janie experienced true love, and, if so, has it changed her?

2. What role does Mrs. Turner play in the novel? Does Hurston use the character to make a universal statement about bigotry?

3. The pear trees, bees, and the horizon occur in several instances in *Their Eyes Were Watching God*. Discuss the significance of these symbols and metaphors in the novel.

4. What is the role of the porch sitters in *Their Eyes Were Watching God*? How do they contribute to the novel?

5. What is the significance of the title *Their Eyes Were Watching God* to the novel? Why would Hurston have chosen it?

Practice Projects

1. Zora Neale Hurston spent approximately two years involved in the literary movement known as the Harlem Renaissance. Research Hurston's activities and her contributions to the Renaissance. Create a timeline to show her activities during the time period.

2. Create a *Their Eyes Were Watching God* Web page. It should serve as a source of review as well as include links to other pertinent areas related to the novel or the author. Include any information which would strengthen a reader's understanding and appreciation of the text. Choose the content, complete research, and design the Web page.

CliffsNotes Resource Center

The learning doesn't need to stop here. CliffsNotes Resource Center shows you the best of the best—links to the best information in print and online about Zora Neale Hurston and works written by and about her. And don't think that this is all we've prepared for you; we've put all kinds of pertinent information at www.cliffsnotes.com. Look for all the terrific resources at your favorite bookstore or local library and on the Internet. When you're online, make your first stop www.cliffsnotes.com, where you'll find more useful information about *Their Eyes Were Watching God.*

Books and Periodicals

While this CliffsNotes book, published by Wiley Publishing, Inc., offers a meaningful interpretation of *Their Eyes Were Watching God,* if you are looking for information about the author and/or related works, you may find these other publications helpful.

HEMENWAY, ROBERT. *Zora Neale Hurston: A Literary Biography.* Urbana: University of Illinois Press, 1977. Hemenway offers a biography of Zora Neale Hurston's life and work. It also includes a foreword by Alice Walker.

HINE, DARLENE CLARK, ed. *Black Women in America: An Historical Encyclopedia.* Vol. 1. Brooklyn, New York: Carlson Publishing, Inc., 1993. 2 vols. This reference book includes biographical information of Hurston's life, themes found in her works, and a summary of *Their Eyes Were Watching God.*

HURSTON, ZORA NEALE. *Dust Tracks on a Road: An Autobiography.* Philadelphia: J. B. Lippincott Company, 1942. Hurston presents an account of her life from her childhood to her life as a writer.

LAMOTHE, DAPHNE. "Voudou Imagery, African American Tradition and Cultural Transformation in Zora Neale Hurston's *Their Eyes Were Watching God.*" *Callaloo* 22 (1999):157–175. Lamothe writes of the significance of "voodoo" signs, symbols, and rituals in Hurston's *Their Eyes Were Watching God.*

SMITH, JESSIE CARNEY, ed. *Notable Black American Women.* Detroit: Gale Research, Inc., 1992. This reference book contains biographical information about Hurston's life as well as themes in her work and a reference section.

WALKER, PIERRE. "Zora Neale Hurston and the Post-Modern Self in *Dust Tracks on a Road*." *African American Review* 32 (Fall, 1998): 387–399. Walker offers a criticism of Hurston's *Dust Tracks on a Road* and its inconsistencies.

Audio

Their Eyes Were Watching God. (2 cassettes, abridged). Caedmon Audio Cassette, 1991. Perhaps the best way to understand the dialect in Hurston's novel is to listen to the text. Narrator Ruby Dee reads the abridged work on these cassettes.

Internet

About.com, `http://classiclit.about.com`—This site serves as a general resource of American literature. It provides links and details related to American literature, as well as a section on Zora Neale Hurston.

PAL: Perspectives in American Literature: A Research and Reference Guide, `http://www.csustan.edu/english/reuben/pal/chap9/9intro.html`—This site contains information on the Harlem Renaissance, including the chronology of important events, novels of the time period, and links to author Zora Neale Hurston.

Index

NOTES

NOTES

NOTES

NOTES

CliffsNotes

LITERATURE NOTES

Absalom, Absalom!
The Aeneid
Agamemnon
Alice in Wonderland
All the King's Men
All the Pretty Horses
All Quiet on the Western Front
All's Well & Merry Wives
American Poets of the 20th Century
American Tragedy
Animal Farm
Anna Karenina
Anthem
Antony and Cleopatra
Aristotle's Ethics
As I Lay Dying
The Assistant
As You Like It
Atlas Shrugged
Autobiography of Ben Franklin
Autobiography of Malcolm X
The Awakening
Babbit
Bartleby & Benito Cereno
The Bean Trees
The Bear
The Bell Jar
Beloved
Beowulf
The Bible
Billy Budd & Typee
Black Boy
Black Like Me
Bleak House
Bless Me, Ultima
The Bluest Eye & Sula
Brave New World
Brothers Karamazov

The Call of the Wild & White Fang
Candide
The Canterbury Tales
Catch-22
Catcher in the Rye
The Chosen
The Color Purple
Comedy of Errors...
Connecticut Yankee
The Contender
The Count of Monte Cristo
Crime and Punishment
The Crucible
Cry, the Beloved Country
Cyrano de Bergerac
Daisy Miller & Turn...Screw
David Copperfield
Death of a Salesman
The Deerslayer
Diary of Anne Frank
Divine Comedy-I. Inferno
Divine Comedy-II. Purgatorio
Divine Comedy-III. Paradiso
Doctor Faustus
Dr. Jekyll and Mr. Hyde
Don Juan
Don Quixote
Dracula
Electra & Medea
Emerson's Essays
Emily Dickinson Poems
Emma
Ethan Frome
The Faerie Queene
Fahrenheit 451
Far from the Madding Crowd
A Farewell to Arms
Farewell to Manzanar
Fathers and Sons
Faulkner's Short Stories

Faust Pt. I & Pt. II
The Federalist
Flowers for Algernon
For Whom the Bell Tolls
The Fountainhead
Frankenstein
The French Lieutenant's Woman
The Giver
Glass Menagerie & Streetcar
Go Down, Moses
The Good Earth
The Grapes of Wrath
Great Expectations
The Great Gatsby
Greek Classics
Gulliver's Travels
Hamlet
The Handmaid's Tale
Hard Times
Heart of Darkness & Secret Sharer
Hemingway's Short Stories
Henry IV Part 1
Henry IV Part 2
Henry V
House Made of Dawn
The House of the Seven Gables
Huckleberry Finn
I Know Why the Caged Bird Sings
Ibsen's Plays I
Ibsen's Plays II
The Idiot
Idylls of the King
The Iliad
Incidents in the Life of a Slave Girl
Inherit the Wind
Invisible Man
Ivanhoe
Jane Eyre
Joseph Andrews
The Joy Luck Club
Jude the Obscure

Julius Caesar
The Jungle
Kafka's Short Stories
Keats & Shelley
The Killer Angels
King Lear
The Kitchen God's Wife
The Last of the Mohicans
Le Morte d'Arthur
Leaves of Grass
Les Miserables
A Lesson Before Dying
Light in August
The Light in the Forest
Lord Jim
Lord of the Flies
The Lord of the Rings
Lost Horizon
Lysistrata & Other Comedies
Macbeth
Madame Bovary
Main Street
The Mayor of Casterbridge
Measure for Measure
The Merchant of Venice
Middlemarch
A Midsummer Night's Dream
The Mill on the Floss
Moby-Dick
Moll Flanders
Mrs. Dalloway
Much Ado About Nothing
My Ántonia
Mythology
Narr. ...Frederick Douglass
Native Son
New Testament
Night
1984
Notes from the Underground

Check Out the All-New CliffsNotes Guides

TECHNOLOGY TOPICS

PERSONAL FINANCE TOPICS

CAREER TOPICS